Vegetable Desserts

Vegetable Desserts: Beyond Carrot Cake and Pumpkin Pie
© 1998 by Elisabeth Schafer and Jeannette L. Miller, RD

Library of Congress Cataloging-in-Publication Data

Schafer, Elisabeth and Miller, Jeannette L.
Vegetable desserts / by Elisabeth Schafer and Jeannette L. Miller, RD

           p.   cm.

Includes index.

ISBN 1-56561-135-7; $16.95

Edited by: Ann L. Burckhardt
Cover Design: Claire Lewis
Text Design & Production: David Enyeart
Art/Production Manager: Claire Lewis
Interior Photographs: John Strange Photography
Printed in Canada

Published by
Chronimed Publishing
P.O. Box 59032
Minneapolis, MN 55459-0032

10   9   8   7   6   5   4   3   2   1

Vegetable Desserts

BEYOND CARROT CAKE AND PUMPKIN PIE

Elisabeth Schafer
&
Jeannette L. Miller, RD

CHRONIMED PUBLISHING

The authors are indebted to Vernon Quinn (Vegetables in the Garden and Their Legends, *J.B. Lippincott, 1942*), *Yann Lovelock* (The Vegetable Book: An Unnatural History, *St. Martin's Press, 1972*), *Nelson Foster and Linda S. Cordell* (Chilies to Chocolate: Food the Americas Gave the World, *University of Arizona Press, 1992*), *and Dave DeWitt and Nancy Gerlach* (The Whole Chile Pepper Book, *Little, Brown, and Co., 1990*) *for some of the folklore and anecdotes recounted herein.*

The following recipes were adapted for use with permission: Beanie Brownies (Mueller Bean Company, Galesburg, ND); Chocolate Chip Pumpkin Cookies (Nebraska Dry Bean Growers Association, Scottsbluff, NE); Apple Bean Spice Cake (Idaho Bean Commission, Boise, ID); Lentil Oatmeal Cookies (USA Dry Pea and Lentil Industry); Chocolate Drop Cookies (Idaho-Washington Dry Pea and Lentil Commission, Moscow, ID); Carrot Raisin Bars (USDA H&G-224); Upside Down Carrot Cake (Dole Fresh Vegetables, Salinas, CA); Cantaloupe Sorbet and Melon Sorbet (Del Monte Fresh Produce, Coral Gables, FL); Watermelon Slyce (National Watermelon Promotion Board, Orlando, FL); Watermelon Cooler (National Watermelon Association, Morven, GA); Hot Ice Cream (Beverly Garber, St. Louis, MO); Rhubarb Cream Pudding, Rhubarb Almond Sauce, Rhubarb Peekaboo, Jellied Rhubarb Pie, Rhubarb Cakeroll with Lemon Cream (Washington Rhubarb Growers Association).

A special thanks goes to Don Hauck, Dickinson, ND, who willingly assisted in testing and evaluating numerous recipes and desserts. We are also indebted to our numerous taste panels for tasting and scoring the trials.

CONTENTS

Introduction

"I say it's spinach, and I say the hell with it."—E. B. White

From artichoke to zucchini, vegetables are receiving renewed emphasis today. Like your mother said, they're good for you. And like generations of children, we still aren't eating our vegetables. Although health organizations recommend at least three servings of vegetables each day, the average American eats two servings or less, and that's even counting French fries.

So if you or your children aren't eating the vegetables you know you should, what's to be done? Buckle down and do your duty? Choke down three mushy, strong-flavored, green "things" a day? No! Eating should be a pleasant part of the day. Many books show how to choose and cook fresh vegetables so they have appealing texture, color, and flavor. But this book shows another way to eat your vegetables and enjoy every bite: Put them in your dessert.

"Don't ruin my dessert. That's the thing I like to eat most." Not to worry. These desserts are so good you won't even know you're eating vegetables.

We Americans crave desserts as much as we avoid vegetables. Dessert, unfortunately, enjoys a favored status in the diet. It is the culmination, the peak, the glorious conclusion of a meal. Symbolically, dessert is a reward. We have learned through experience that dessert is highly desirable. Rare is the child or adult who refuses dessert. So, let's put our love affair with dessert to work for us.

As nutritionists we are often asked if we allow our families to have dessert. Of course, we do. But we also have a silent motto: "If you're going to eat dessert, make it count." So, we make desserts that are more than sweet and gooey. They are sweet, gooey, and packed with vitamins, minerals, and fiber. We also reduce the fat and sugar in our desserts so cleverly that no one knows some of the calories are missing. What your taste buds can't tell, your waistline can proudly show.

This book is for both the person with vegetable-phobia and the vegetable-lover.

Everyone is familiar with the classic vegetable desserts pumpkin pie and carrot cake. This book will give you recipes for these classics (updated to reduce the fat and calories), plus a host of new and unusual ideas for making vegetables come to life in your desserts. When we served Autumn Gold (page 174) to a group of friends and asked them to guess the ingredients, they asked for seconds and didn't care what the ingredients were. When we serve the dramatic Danish Carrot Pudding (page 36) at Christmas dinner each year, flaming it at the table in front of the guests, no one suspects that the rich tasting dessert they are enjoying is full of carrots and potatoes.

Cabbage in a cookie? Celery in a cake? Come with us on an adventure in eating that will help you combine healthful eating with delightful dining. Find out how to make candy with pinto beans or sweet potatoes, and ice cream with jalapeño peppers or yams. Dessert has never been so good (we promise) and so good for you!

WHAT IS A VEGETABLE, ANYWAY?

Certain questions defy conclusive answers. All explanations aside, the debates continue generation after generation. If a tree falls in a forest and no one is there to hear, does the falling tree make a sound? Is the tomato a fruit or a vegetable? Is sweet corn a grain or a vegetable?

Disagreements persist because we have more than one definition for vegetable, and for fruit, for that matter.

In the strict botanical sense, vegetable refers to the edible portion of an herbaceous plant. An herbaceous plant dies at the end of the season and must be restarted from seed. Raspberry bushes, apple trees, and strawberry plants, for example, "survive" the winter. When spring comes they put forth new leaves from the parent plant, not from a sprouting seed. Thus the edible portions of these plants are not called vegetables.

Edible portions of herbaceous plants include roots (carrots and turnips), stems (asparagus and celery), leaves (lettuce and spinach), flowers (broccoli and cauliflower), seeds (sweet corn, green peas), and fruits. Fruits!? In our careless use of language we create confusion. Some fruits are vegetables!

Botanically speaking, fruit is the ovary of a plant, enclosing the seed or seeds. So fruits include not only apricot, plum, and apple, but also pumpkin, cucumber, green bean, and green pepper. The fruit is a plant part, just as are the leaf, stem and root. Thoroughly confused?

We could use the culinary definition for fruits and vegetables. Popularly, we use the word *fruit* only for the sweet, succulent, pulpy ovaries of plants. Then we use the word *vegetable* for edible plant ovaries that are not sweet such as the cucumber, bean, or tomato. We also use the word *vegetable* for all other parts of a plant that we eat—the root, stems, leaves, flowers, and seeds.

Both the botanical and the culinary definitions of vegetables are all-inclusive. Rhubarb is a vegetable. Melons are vegetables. Tomatoes are a vegetable. In fact, the U.S. Supreme Court says so.

In 1883 the United States collected tariffs on imported vegetables. Imported fruits, by contrast, were duty-free. Naturally, tomato shippers claimed the tomato was a fruit and therefore not subject to import fees. Just as naturally, the customs staff were eager to claim the tomato was a vegetable and subject to tariff. Such a dispute could only be decided in the courts, and the case reached the highest bench. The Supreme Court's decision was unanimous. According to the botanical definition, the tomato was both a fruit and a vegetable. However, the court concluded that since tomatoes were generally served with the savory portions of a meal—the soup and meat courses—and were not served as a dessert course, the tomato was not a fruit, but a vegetable.

Throughout this book we use the botanical definition of vegetable, which includes some "fruits." So you'll find recipes for pumpkin and peppers, rhubarb and rutabaga, tomato and turnip, cantaloupe and cucumber, and other delightful "veggies." You'll also find recipes for the special class of vegetables known as legumes.

VEGETABLES ARE NOTHING NEW.

Humans have been eating vegetables from the beginning. Hunter-gatherer groups of people ate the leaves, stems, and roots of the plants growing around them. In time, humans began to cultivate those plants that they found most desirable. Plant historians cannot find a time when humans were not growing and eating potatoes, greens, corn, beans, garlic, and several other of today's popular vegetables.

Vegetables were basic foods among peoples all over the world until the modern age. Commonly used vegetables in Africa included melons, squashes, and cucumbers. The diet for peoples of the Americas was grounded in maize, beans, potatoes, tomatoes, and squashes. Asia's multitudes incorporated large amounts of vegetables in their traditional diets. Popular vegetables among Europeans and American colonists were carrots, cabbage, celery, and lettuce.

Vegetables, even more than meat or dairy products, have been at the core of the human diet. In times of famine and war, people have subsisted on wild greens and roots. In fact, it may be the very basic nature of vegetables that has made them seem to lack glamour, interest, and desirability.

THEIR DECLINING FORTUNES

Beginning in the 19th century and continuing through most of the 20th century in North America, vegetables became a minor part of the diet. One reason may be the migratory nature of Americans. Spreading westward, explorers, adventurers, and pioneers did not stay in one place long enough to cultivate vegetables. And since vegetables are perishable and heavy with water, they didn't go into the rations bag for journeys.

A second reason for the declining fortunes of vegetables may have been the rise in prosperity accompanied by increased use of the foods associated with wealth: meat and dairy products. For centuries these luxurious foods had symbolized status. Vegetables were foods for the poor masses. As our society prospered we relegated vegetables to second-class status in meals. We found ourselves eating vegetables only because we thought we should, and not because we viewed vegetables as desirable in their own right. Only in the latter years of the 20th century are vegetables beginning to come into their own once again as dietary stars.

A VITAL FOOD

If there is a perfect food, it's probably vegetables. No other category of human food has such diversity of choices, range of flavors, and brilliance of colors. And no other category of foods more nearly fits today's need for foods low in fat, high in fiber, and rich in the vitamins, minerals, and phytochemicals that reduce risk for the chronic degenerative diseases that plague developed nations. Research studies have linked eating vegetables to reduced risk for heart disease and certain types of cancer. Diets rich in vegetables can help reduce high blood pressure. Nutrition scientists agree on at least this one piece of advice: Eat more vegetables!

Unfortunately, this unanimous call for eating more vegetables has not been translated into action. Americans are eating far less than the recommended amounts. The minimum recommendation, agreed upon by nearly all health and nutrition professionals, is 5 servings a day of fruits and vegetables in total, divided into 3 servings of vegetables and 2 of fruit.

In contrast, the National Cancer Institute says Americans are averaging less than 2 servings of vegetables a day, and only 23 percent of Americans eat the full 5 servings a day of fruits and vegetables.

Why are we avoiding vegetables? The National Cancer Institute thinks there are three reasons: convenience, cost, and reluctance to try new items. We want vegetables (and other foods, for that matter) that are quick and easy to prepare. The astounding success of peeled mini carrots shows that we will eat vegetables if they are ready to eat.

Contrary to popular opinion, vegetables are very inexpensive. Whole, raw potatoes cost 20 cents per pound, compared to potato chips at $2.60 per pound. A big, crispy, sweet carrot costs less than a tiny candy bar or a can of soft drink.

Studies with preschoolers have found that children usually need to taste a new food three times before they like it. Adults are probably not much different. Trying new vegetables, prepared in simple, unique ways, could help us want more of them in our daily diet.

WHY WE DON'T EAT ENOUGH VEGETABLES

We think there are other reasons why Americans aren't eating enough vegetables to be healthy.

Flavor: Carelessly cooked vegetables such as cabbage and greens have strong flavors. Some adults were forced to eat a vegetable during childhood that was cooked in a way they didn't like. This experience turned them against the offending vegetable forever. Actually, a properly cooked vegetable has a mild, pleasant taste. If you are brave enough to try our Kraut Crisps (containing cabbage, page 27) or Curious Lemon Cake (containing spinach, page 68), you will find the flavors subtle. In fact, if you didn't know, you probably wouldn't be able to guess that the luscious dessert you were eating contained a vegetable with all its whole-some goodness.

Boredom: How were the vegetables that you ate yesterday prepared? Dumped from a can or plastic pouch and boiled? Yes, we thought so! Less imagination and care are given to cooking and serving vegetables than any other class of food in our menus. Your recipe file is probably stuffed with dessert and main dish recipes. If you have a file for vegetable recipes, its contents are probably pretty skimpy. And if vegetables are cooked and served the same old way every day, well, who's going to get excited about eating them?

Although there are scores of vegetables in a variety of colors, flavors, shapes, and textures, only a few are eaten at all frequently. In our experiences as guest nutrition teachers for school-age children, many students in each classroom have never seen, let alone tasted, kohlrabi, turnips, eggplant, bean sprouts, or even broccoli or zucchini.

According to a 1992 study by the National Cancer Institute, the eight most popular vegetables in the United States, based on frequency of consumption, are (1) green salad, (2) fried potatoes, (3) potatoes prepared in other ways, (4) green beans, (5) peas, (6) corn, (7) tomatoes, and (8) tomato sauce.

So unimaginative! And several of these popular vegetables—corn, iceberg lettuce, cucumber—don't provide much, nutritionally-speaking, other than fiber. Conspicuously absent are the winter squashes, outstanding sources of carotenes (vitamin A). Our list of the most nutritious vegetables would be quite different and would include sweet potatoes, pumpkin, carrots, broccoli, cabbage, spinach, and potato without added fat.

To tempt you to go beyond the ordinary, the recipes in this book will invite you into delicious adventures with beets, jicama, parsnips, split peas, and other less-used vegetables, as well as the familiar carrot, tomato, and potato.

BUYING VEGETABLES

The good cook uses the best ingredients. When vegetables fail to please, it is often because the cook has tried to get by with lower quality produce. Highest quality does not mean highest price. Use the following ideas to help you become a dis-criminating shopper, so you can get the best quality at the best price.

This book contains a shopping and selection guide for each of the 24 featured vegetables. For example, learn what to look for when choosing a winter squash (page 162). Learn how to judge the ripeness of a melon (page 82), or how to store tomatoes so they will ripen with the most flavor (page 201).

Although each vegetable has its own unique signals of freshness and flavor, here are some general principles on choosing vegetables that will please your family and friends, enhance your reputation as a good cook, and not strain your wallet.

VEGETABLES TASTE AND LOOK
BEST DURING THEIR SEASON

Modern transportation and storage have made most vegetables available year-round, even in northern climates. For a price, you can eat fresh tomatoes in January or watermelon in December. But make no mistake, the flavor is rarely as rich as in August. The varieties of perishable vine vegetables that are grown for out-of-season marketing are chosen for their ability to retain an attractive appearance despite shipping and storage, not for their flavor.

In general, vegetables have the greatest flavoral and textural quality when they go directly from garden to table. With a few exceptions, the sweetest vegetables have ripened in the warmth of the sun. The exceptions are some "winter" vegetables that become sweeter after a light frost, for example, pumpkin and rutabaga.

Another advantage of buying vegetables in season is that is when the price is lowest. On the next page is a chart of seasonal availability to help you get first-rate quality at the most reasonable cost.

VEGETABLES SHOULD BE FIRM,
NOT FLABBY, CRISP, NOT WILTED.

Dehydration is the enemy of vegetable quality. Vegetables are like sponges full of water. The water is what makes them crisp, juicy, low-calorie, and delicious. Lettuce is 96 percent water. A carrot is 88 percent water. Even a baked potato is 75 percent water.

Solid vegetables like peas, green peppers, celery, and cucumbers should be firm. If they are flabby or soft, they have lost too much water and with the water, their flavor. Choose vegetables that haven't started to dry out.

Leafy vegetables like lettuce and greens should be crisp. Wilted or yellowing leaves are a signal the vegetable is thirsty. While soaking in water might return some degree of crispness, the flavor and nutrients that were lost cannot be restored. Choose leafy vegetables that are crisp and well colored.

VEGETABLES AT THEIR PEAKS

Vegetables (rows): Beans, green · Beets · Cabbage · Cantaloupe · Carrots · Celery · Corn · Cucumbers · Honeydew · Jicama · Onions, dry · Parsnips · Peas · Peppers · Potatoes · Pumpkin · Rhubarb · Rutabagas · Spinach · Squash · Sweet Potatoes · Tomatoes · Turnips · Watermelon

Months (columns): JAN · FEB · MAR · APR · MAY · JUNE · JULY · AUG · SEPT · OCT · NOV · DEC

Legend:

PEAK SUPPLY ❧

FAIR SUPPLY ❧

LOW SUPPLY OR UNAVAILABLE ❧

Watch out for soft spots on vegetables. These are signs of coming rot and decay. Reject vegetables that show signs of mildew or mold.

NATURAL COLOR IS A GUIDE TO NUTRITIVE VALUE.
The deeper the color, the more concentrated the vitamins. The carotenoids, which turn to vitamin A in your body, are brightly-colored compounds. In fact, they are often used as natural additives to give color to foods such as cheese and pudding mixes. Pure beta-carotene, one of the most familiar and abundant carotenoids, is deep orange. The more intense the yellow or orange in a vegetable, the richer it is in vitamin A.

Lycopene, the carotenoid in tomatoes, is a maverick. Instead of conforming with the rest of the carotenoid family and being deep orange or yellow, it is deep red in its pure form.

Green vegetables such as spinach, broccoli, and green peppers are also excellent sources of carotenoids, but the deep yellow and orange pigments are hidden beneath the dominant green chlorophyll pigment.

Vegetables with small areas of discoloration or imperfect shapes are not necessarily of lower quality. Organically-grown vegetables do not always have the picture-perfect look of vegetables grown with sprays. Choose vegetables not just for their looks, but for their firmness, crispness, and depth of color. Remember that sometimes looks can be deceiving, and appearance is not a reliable guide to flavor.

WHERE TO FIND THE BEST VEGETABLES
While supermarkets contain some excellent vegetables, there is another source of these jewels of the diet. Farmers' markets, a centuries-old idea reborn in the last half of the 20th century, are places where you can get vegetables grown close to home. Often you can buy vegetables so fresh they were still in the field or garden only an hour or two before you purchased them. The vegetables you buy direct from the small farmer are often of superior flavor and quality, just because they did not have to endure the rigors of mechanized harvest and long-distance transportation.

Farmers' markets are proliferating across America. Any list of local markets would soon be outdated because new ones are growing to meet the booming demand. One listing of state-by-state and community-by-community farmers' markets can be found on the Internet at

http://www.bpe.com/food/farmers/farmers.html

The makers of this list frankly admit that it is incomplete. We can attest that the list is incomplete because the 10-year-old farmers' market in the city where one of us lives is not listed!

To find the farmers' market nearest you, you might search the Internet for state-specific listings. And there are hundreds. But you might also watch for announcements in your local newspaper, ask around, or call the local chamber of commerce or your state's department of agriculture.

FROZEN AND CANNED VEGETABLES

Contrary to popular belief, frozen and canned vegetables usually contain more vitamins than do the fresh vegetables in the urban supermarket. Why? Most vitamins are fairly fragile. The minute a vegetable is picked from the garden or the farmer's field, the vitamins begin to disappear. If the vegetable is stored properly—in cool darkness, with little oxygen—then the rate of vitamin loss is slowed.

Vegetables for the supermarket are usually harvested and shipped long distances. By the time you purchase them, these vegetables have been away from their fields for several days. By contrast, the vegetables in a can or frozen package were usually processed within hours of their harvest, thus preserving more of the nutrients.

Choose cans that are not dented. Small dents probably have not compromised the seal, but you can't be sure. If dents have weakened the vacuum seal, the food is not safe to eat.

Frozen vegetables should be used immediately after they have been thawed. For that reason, choose packages that are frozen hard. Packages that are soft have already begun to defrost. Packages that are stained or covered with frost have been thawed and refrozen. While in most cases the food is still safe to eat, the quality is greatly lessened. The texture, flavor, and nutrient value have all been reduced.

DRIED VEGETABLES

One of the recipes in this book calls for sun-dried tomatoes—Habanero Surprise, page 110. Dehydrated vegetables have a chewy texture that can add a new dimension to your cooking and eating. Dehydrated or freeze-dried vegetables are convenient and can be stored for a long time. But, and this is a big "but," they are not as nutritious as fresh, frozen, or canned vegetables. The reason is those fragile vitamins. Most of the vitamins are readily destroyed by exposure to air, and since that is what dehydrating is all about, the vitamin content of dried vegetables is small.

INGREDIENT SAVVY

Many cooks, regardless of their culinary skills, will avoid a recipe because their cupboard doesn't have the ingredients listed in the recipe. With many homes and apartments having smaller kitchens and limited storage, cooking can appear quite limited from the standpoint of both equipment and ingredients. This needn't be a problem if you consider the substitutions you can make that will give you the taste and texture the recipe was intended to have.

Likewise, those that are cooking for one or two sometimes avoid recipes and cookbooks because they feel the recipes create too much food for their household. The section on pan sizes gives pointers on how to reduce recipe sizes to a yield compatible with your household.

THE EGGS IN OUR BASKET

Eggs, a basic ingredient in desserts, are a compact package of high quality protein and an important source of vitamins. Supermarket eggs are graded AA or A. There is very little difference in the two grades. Eggs are also graded by size, determined by weight—small, medium, large, extra large, and jumbo. From one size to the next there is a difference of 3 ounces per dozen eggs. Baking recipes are generally written for large eggs. To give you a perspective on the sizes—5 large eggs equal about 1 cup, compared to 7 small eggs to measure 1 cup. The recipes in this book were all tested with large eggs.

Several brands of egg substitutes are now available at the supermarket. Take time to read the label and know what you are buying. Some brands are egg whites with yellow coloring added; others may have fat added and indeed may have more calories than a regular egg although the cholesterol has been removed. The label will give you the information to estimate an egg equivalent. With most recipes these products are satisfactory substitutes for whole fresh eggs. If you are looking for the volume and airiness of egg whites, however, use real eggs. The fat is entirely in the yolk. The egg white is fat free.

EXTRACT OR FLAVORING—WHICH TO CHOOSE?

Stocking your pantry with a wide variety of extracts and flavorings is a financial and storage space investment, especially if you are the occasional cook. Before you buy, consider what types of baking and cooking you will do most often. Generally, for baked desserts, a flavoring will blend the flavors of the ingredients together nicely. If you will add the flavoring agent after the cooking or baking is completed, then you should use an extract. This is why we have used both extracts and flavorings throughout this collection of vegetable dessert recipes.

If you are trying a new flavoring and are uncertain how it will affect the dessert, start with 1½ teaspoons of the flavoring for a standard size batch of cookies or a 9-inch by 13-inch cake. Use extracts and flavors alone or in combination with one another to produce a more well-rounded, delicate flavor. Use amounts that yield a delicately pleasing, but not overpowering, flavor and aroma.

Our collection of recipes includes some flavorings you might find unusual. For example, Zip Chip Bars, page 55, uses black walnut flavoring. When you taste the bars, you won't detect black walnut, yet that flavoring is the key ingredient that blends the flavors of all the other ingredients to give a subtly delicious dessert.

SUBSTITUTING—AVOIDING AN
EXTRA JAUNT TO THE GROCERY STORE

Extracts can be useful substitutes for other ingredients. If, for example, a recipe calls for grated lemon rind and you don't have a fresh lemon on hand, ½ teaspoon lemon extract can be substituted for 1 teaspoon of grated rind. Because pure lemon extract is made from the lemon oil in the rind, the flavor in the final product will be practically the same. Knowing this can save you a trip to the store or save the disappointment of not cooking a recipe because you don't have what the recipe calls for.

Oat bran can be difficult to find in some grocery stores. You can substitute steel-cut oats, sometimes sold as Scotch oats or Irish oats, or even rolled oats. These terms refer to how the oats are processed and how thinly cut, steamed, or rolled flat they are. A recipe made with any of these in place of oat bran will have more texture and flavor. You could also use quick or instant oats although the texture, flavor, and fiber will be lessened.

PIE SHELL POINTERS

Whether the deciding factor be time or inexperience, today's cook often uses a commercial pie shell. A problem can occur when you discover that the amount of pie filling (or dessert) is far greater than the pastry shell will hold. To avoid this problem, read the label carefully and take a close look at the shell when you are in the store. For instance, if the pie shell you pick up in the frozen food case looks skimpy and less than an inch deep, it will likely be too small for a 9-inch pie filling. If you already have the shell in your freezer, prepare only half the recipe or make two pies. In a one-person household, cutting a recipe in half can be a great way to bake a small dessert in one of the shallow pie shells.

Regardless of what the label says, if a pie shell looks skimpy, put it back and search out one that says "deep dish." To measure a pie pan or a pastry crust, measure the top inside diameter, not across the top edge to edge of the pan. Pans and commercial pie shells vary from 8 inches to 10 inches and from 1 inch to 2 inches deep! Check out the recipe before you begin so you don't face disappointment at the end.

Another comment about pie crusts. Baking time will vary depending on the type of material the pan is made from. Pans that are dark, ovenproof glass, or enamelware can reduce baking time by one fourth. A shiny aluminum pan reflects heat away and is more likely to require the full baking time stated in the recipe. If you notice the edge of the crust is browning too quickly, crimp three or four aluminum foil strips and place them around the edge to reflect heat away from the crust and slow down the browning.

THE UNIQUE BOTTOM LINE—CREATIVITY

Part of the fun of cooking is creating. Being creative not only with flavors but also with ingredients that add vitamins, minerals, and fiber is a real dividend. Some of the special pie crusts we have used in our collection capitalize on this opportunity. A word of warning—don't try to improvise with these recipes. The proportion of fat to flour and water has been carefully worked out. The most common reason for poor results with pie crusts is failure to strictly follow the technique or the ingredients as stated in the recipe.

Oatmeal crust adds soluble fiber. The bonus is the subtle, nutty-like flavor it lends to several pies in our collection. Find it used with Mint Julep Pie, page 103.

Sweet potato is a very colorful, sweet, root vegetable that lends itself to a radiant crust, packed with healthful beta-carotene. Try this unusual pastry crust with Sweet Potato Custard Pie, page 193 and Sweet Pizza, page 191.

Cornmeal lends color and chewy texture to a pastry crust. Try our Cornmeal Crust with Maple Sweet Potato Pie, page 194, then try it with other favorite pie recipes.

Whatever crust and filling you use, for optimal flavor and pleasure, do serve any pie the day you bake it, unless you plan to freeze it.

YOGURT CHEESE

This unique new ingredient is so easy to use and so versatile that a food company will probably soon begin marketing it at convenience food prices. In the meantime, you can make it easily at home for pennies. Yogurt cheese is a creamy, fat-free ingredient in Creamy Chocolate Frosting for Chocolate Surprise Cake, page 29, and Glorious Rhubarb Meringue Pie, page 154.

Yogurt Cheese

1 paper coffee filter, basket type
2 3/4 inch x 3 inch
strainer or colander

2-quart glass or stainless steel
mixing bowl
16-ounce carton plain, nonfat yogurt
that contains no gelatin

Place filter in strainer basket and set over bowl. Spoon yogurt into filter. Cover loosely with plastic wrap and refrigerate 4 to 12 hours. Varying brands will need different lengths of time for draining. When approximately 1 cup of whey has drained off, yogurt cheese is what remains in the filter. Spoon it into a container and refrigerate. Discard whey.

DRY BEANS, LENTILS, AND PEAS

Legume purees are convenience ingredients you can make in advance and have on hand for quick dessert-making when the mood strikes. Purees are used in several recipes in the beans, lentils, and peas sections.

Wash all dry legumes before beginning and sort out bits of straw, stones, or broken beans if necessary. Place lentils, split peas, or beans in saucepan with water, according to the chart below. For lentils and split peas, add salt and margarine if desired, bring to a boil, reduce heat, and simmer, covered. For pinto and great northern beans, bring to a boil and cook 2 minutes. Remove from heat, cover, and let stand 1 to 2 hours. (This presoaking speeds up cooking time greatly.) Discard soaking water and add fresh water to the soaked beans. Add salt and margarine at this time, if desired. Again bring the beans to a boil, reduce heat, cover, and simmer until the beans are tender.

BEAN	WATER	SALT	MARGARINE	COOKING TIME	YIELD
Pinto/Great Northern	4 cups	1 tsp.	1 Tbsp.	2 hours	4 cups
2 cups=1 pound					
Lentils	5 cups	1 tsp.	1 Tbsp.	30-45 minutes	5 cups
2 1/4 cups=1 pound					
Split Peas	6 cups	1 tsp.	1 Tbsp.	1 hour	8 cups
2 1/4 cups=1 pound					

Test for tenderness in one of two ways. Prick with a fork or blow gently on a bean and see if the skin curls. While still warm, puree beans, lentils, or peas in blender, or food processor, or mash by hand. Store in a covered container in the refrigerator for up to one 1 week or in the freezer for 6 months.

EQUIPMENT SAVVY,
OR RATTLING THE POTS AND PANS

Only the most dedicated cook has every pan shape and size on the pantry shelves. Most of us have neither the space nor the desire to have more than three or four sizes of baking pans. So where is one to turn when the recipe calls for a size we don't have? Learn to substitute!

A rule of thumb for successful baking is: fill the pan "two-thirds full" with batter. Measure the amount of water the pan will hold, then measure your batter to be two-thirds of its total volume. To bake half a recipe designed for a 9 inch x 13 inch cake pan, choose an 8-inch square pan. For a slightly thinner product, choose a 9-inch round pan.

If you have a uniquely-shaped baking pan, found at a gift shop, antique store, or grandma's cupboard, you can identify its size by measuring across the top between the inside edges only, not to the outer edges.

QUICK ACTION

If you use your microwave oven extensively, you know what items will cook well with its unique heat and speed. If you only heat or thaw foods in the microwave, you may not be familiar with the names and wattages of the various power levels. Unfortunately, the industry has never standardized microwave oven wattage and power levels. The recipes in this book refer to "high power," "30 percent power," and "low power." You will have to judge how those terms best apply to your own equipment. Check the owner's guide/cookbook that came with the appliance. It is worth doing this bit of homework because it is all too easy to overcook with a microwave oven.

Beans

HISTORY

Beans are one of the great nourishers of humankind. Beans have been used for human food since prehistoric times and everywhere on the earth's surface. They were a staple of ancient American peoples and were eaten in bronze-age settlements in Europe. They have been found in sand-covered Egyptian tombs. Asians created many unusual ways to eat beans, which have now become popular in western nations.

In Homer's *Iliad*, cakes made from beans were offered to the gods and goddesses to obtain divine favor. Egyptian priests believed that human souls might transmigrate into beans after death. For that reason the bean was greatly revered and was sometimes used as a funeral plant. In pre-imperial Rome, beans were used as counters in voting. Today we still find beans useful as markers or counters in playing games.

Throughout the Americas, archeologists are constantly digging up dried beans in the sites of ancient inhabitations. In Mexico, the Aztec kings received an annual tribute from their subjects of 5,000 tons of beans.

When the conquering Spaniards established a new city in Peru, they named it Lima, meaning "city of kings." Soon they were exporting to Europe a wonderful bean they found growing there. Naturally, the Europeans quickly named the new food the lima bean.

Beans were a novel food for the early English colonists in North America. Captain John Smith, eating the first beans of his life at a ceremonial dinner with Chief Powhatan at Jamestown, declared they were "sweet as hazelnuts." The Massachusetts Bay Colony quickly put the unfamiliar food to a nonfood use. When they voted, they used white beans to mean yes and black beans to mean no.

In Japanese mythology the story is told of the creator who was so pleased with the final three divinities created that he named them Goddess of the Sun, God of the Moon, and God of the Sea. Unfortunately, the new God of the Sea didn't like water and he rebelled. Angrily the creator banished him. The former God of the Sea had no place of his own. He roamed the earth, but soon grew bored. On a visit to his sister the Goddess of the Sun, he caused so much trouble she threw him out. Hungry and homeless, he asked his other sister, the Goddess of the Earth, for something to eat. Never satisfied, he didn't like what she provided. Ever willful and violent, he killed the Goddess of the Earth and stamped on her body until it sank below the soft, rich soil. From her body sprang the five plants which mean life to the Japanese people: beans, soybeans, rice, millet, and barley.

Beans were often associated with witchcraft. Jack and the Beanstalk is a good example of the folklore of magic associated with beans. Scottish witches rode through the skies, not on broomsticks, but on beanstalks. You could scare ghosts away by spitting beans at them.

A more practical use of beans long ago was to cure toothache and small pox. Just bury a roasted bean and you would soon be well.

Beans were good fortune-tellers. In China, three soybeans soaked in sesame oil were used to predict the future. In Italy, girls placed a dark bean and a light-colored bean in a bag and shook it. Then they drew out one of the beans. The girl who drew a dark bean would have a husband who was poor. A light bean predicted a rich and happy life.

Beans were such an important crop that in some countries stealing beans from another's field was a capital offense.

Beans are so popular that they have spawned innumerable popular sayings and riddles. Someone who is "full of beans" enjoys high spirits and well-being. "If you shake a poor man by the collar, you will hear the beans rattle in his belly." A person who "knows how many beans make five" is very wise. An old proverb says that "hunger makes hard beans sweet." "Three blue beans in a blue bladder" is a challenging, traditional tongue-twister. Try it!

SEASON

Beans are never really out of season. Green or snap beans are available in super-markets all year long, but the best supply and lowest prices occur during the summer growing season. Dry beans are always available and inexpensive.

One reason for beans' popularity is that they can be eaten two distinctly different ways. When you use green beans, you eat the tiny, immature seeds along with the pod. If allowed to mature, the seeds grow large and dry. Dried beans can be saved for cooking weeks, months, or even years later.

QUALITY AND STORAGE

Green or Snap Beans: Choose crisp, slender pods that are bright green, firm, and free of blemish. Avoid thick pods and those that show bulging seeds. These are overly mature and will be tough and less flavorful. Store unwashed beans in a plastic bag in the refrigerator. The sugars will begin turning to starch and the beans will begin to get "rust spots" after a few days, so use them as soon as possible.

Dried: Look for dried beans with a bright color. Faded color means the beans are old and will take much longer to cook. Uniform size is important for uniform cooking. Naturally, smaller beans cook faster than large ones. Inspect dry beans, removing any broken beans or foreign materials. Rinse dried beans in cold water before use. Dried beans will keep indefinitely in a cool, dark cupboard; but the longer they have been stored, the tougher they become and the longer it will take to cook them to tenderness.

Tofu: Often called bean curd, it is a delicate-flavored white product of soybeans. Tofu comes in bulk and in aseptically-packaged individual blocks. Either way, it should be kept moist in water. Be guided by the freshness date stamped on the package. Bulk tofu won't have a freshness date, so use your nose as a guide. If you can smell a sour odor, it's too old. At home, store tofu in the refrigerator. Rinse the bulk tofu and place it in a clean container of fresh, cold water. Keep it covered, and change the water daily.

NUTRITIONAL QUALITY

Beans are high in protein content. In South and Central America, in tropical Africa, in Asia, and among vegetarians the world over, beans are the major source of protein. Beans are also very rich in iron and dietary fiber. There is hardly another plant food that is such a nutritional bargain. Fat-free and cholesterol-free, high in fiber, a good source of iron and protein, beans are the ideal food to meet today's dietary guidelines and today's dietary concerns. One cup of cooked dried beans provides 23 percent of the Daily Value for protein; 22 percent of the Daily Value for iron; and 48 percent of the Daily Value for dietary fiber. The immature green or snap beans are a good source of vitamin C and beta-carotene. Once dried, however, beans have very little of these unstable vitamins.

The infamous gas of beans is caused by the presence of oligosaccharides (large carbohydrate molecules), which are not digested well. The oligosaccharides can be largely eliminated during cooking by two important steps—discard all soaking and cooking water and cook the beans thoroughly, until they are really soft and tender. The oligosaccharides tend to leach out into the cooking water, so changing the water often and pouring it down the drain can encourage more leaching. You don't want to use the cooking water—it's loaded with the problematic compounds.

For additional desserts incorporating beans, see Habanero Surprise, page 110, and Pumpkin Plus Cheesecake, page 140. And see directions for cooking dried beans— page XX.

Iced Spiced Cookies

Has your family tried them?

4 DOZEN

Nonstick vegetable cooking spray

3/4 cup cooked pinto beans

1/2 cup shortening

1 cup brown sugar

2 eggs

3/4 cup applesauce

2 1/4 cups sifted all-purpose flour, divided

1 teaspoon baking soda

1 teaspoon baking powder

1/2 teaspoon salt

1/2 teaspoon cinnamon

1/2 teaspoon cloves

1/2 teaspoon ginger

1/2 teaspoon nutmeg

3/4 cup walnuts

1/2 cup raisins

Browned Butter Icing (recipe follows)

Preheat oven to 375°. Spray cookie sheets with cooking spray and set aside. Warm the beans, place in blender or food processor, and puree. Cream shortening, sugar, and eggs. Add applesauce and pureed pintos. Continue beating until fluffy. Add dry ingredients to 2 cups flour and sift. Add the flour mixture to the creamy mixture 1/3 at a time, beating until smooth. Coat nuts and raisins with remaining 1/4 cup flour. Add to the batter. Drop by teaspoonfuls on baking sheet. Bake for 15 to 20 minutes or until lightly browned. Remove from pan and cool. Ice with Browned Butter Icing (below).

Browned Butter Icing

3 tablespoons stick butter

2 cups powdered sugar, sifted

1/2 teaspoon ground ginger

2 tablespoons + 1 teaspoon milk

3/4 teaspoon vanilla extract

Brown butter in small skillet over medium heat until delicately browned. Blend in sugar and ginger. Stir in milk, not adding the last teaspoon unless it is needed to create a good spreading consistency. Add vanilla and beat until smooth.

Nutrition Facts (per serving)

Serving size 1 cookie (30g); Servings per recipe 48; Calories 105; Calories from Fat 36; Total Fat 4g (6% DV); Saturated Fat 1g (5% DV); Cholesterol 11mg (4% DV); Vitamin A 1% DV; Vitamin C 0; Sodium 60mg (2% DV); Total Carbohydrate 16g (5% DV); Dietary Fiber 1g (4% DV); Protein 1g; Calcium 1% DV; Iron 3% DV

Big Bite Bars
Great for those after school snack attacks.

48 SERVINGS

Nonstick vegetable cooking spray
2 cups all-purpose flour
2 cups sugar
2 teaspoons baking powder
1 teaspoon baking soda
2 teaspoons cinnamon
1/2 teaspoon nutmeg

2 cups pinto beans, mashed, warm
3/4 cup applesauce
2 eggs
3/4 cup peanut butter chips
1 cup walnuts, chopped
Peanut Butter Frosting (recipe below)

Preheat oven to 350°. Spray a 15 1/2-inch x 10-inch x 1-inch pan with cooking spray and set aside. Sift together dry ingredients in large bowl. Add mashed pinto beans, applesauce, and eggs. Mix thoroughly. Stir in peanut butter chips and nuts. Spread in pan. Bake for 20 to 25 minutes or until no imprint remains when lightly touched. Allow to cool, then frost with Peanut Butter Frosting. Cut into 48 bars (6 by 8).

NOTE: These bars freeze well.

Peanut Butter Frosting

1/2 cup creamy peanut butter
2 cups powdered sugar, sifted

7 tablespoons skim milk
1 teaspoon vanilla extract

Beat peanut butter and powdered sugar together. Add milk and stir in vanilla.

Nutrition Facts (per serving)

Serving size 1 bar (42g); Servings per recipe 48; Calories 130; Calories from Fat 36; Total Fat 4g (6% DV); Saturated Fat 0 DV; Cholesterol 11mg (4% DV); Vitamin A 0; Vitamin C 0; Sodium 54mg (2% DV); Total Carbohydrate 21g (7% DV); Dietary Fiber 1g (4% DV); Protein 4g; Calcium 2%; Iron 4%

Beanie Brownies

Not to be confused with Brownie beanies, but loved just the same.

24 SERVINGS

Nonstick vegetable cooking spray	*1 egg*
20-ounce package low-fat brownie mix	*1 cup bean puree (see page XXI)*
1/3 cup skim milk	*1/2 cup chocolate chips*
1/4 cup margarine, softened	*1/2 cup walnuts, chopped*

Preheat oven to 350°. Spray a 9-inch x 13-inch pan with cooking spray; set aside. In large mixing bowl combine all ingredients except chocolate chips and nuts. Mix thoroughly by hand or with an electric mixer. Fold in nuts and chips. Spread the thick batter into prepared pan and bake for 20 to 25 minutes Brownies will pull away slightly from edge of pan when done and will spring back when touched lightly with fingertip. Cool one hour before cutting into 24 bars (4 by 6).

Nutrition Facts (per serving)

Serving size 1 bar (57g); Servings per recipe 24; Calories 165; Calories from Fat 18; Total Fat 2g (3% DV); Saturated Fat 1g (5% DV); Cholesterol 10mg (3% DV); Vitamin A 2% DV; Vitamin C 0; Sodium 150mg (6% DV); Total Carbohydrate 33g (11% DV); Dietary Fiber 2g (8% DV); Protein 3g; Calcium 2% DV; Iron 7% DV

Pinto Bean Fudge

An old-fashioned delight.

96 PIECES

Nonstick vegetable cooking spray

2 cups cooked pinto beans, warm

1/3 cup margarine or butter, melted

1 cup unsweetened cocoa

4 ounces unsweetened baking chocolate, melted

1 tablespoon vanilla extract

2 pounds powdered sugar, sifted

1 cup chopped walnuts

Spray a 9-inch x 13-inch pan with cooking spray; set aside. Mash or puree pinto beans. Add butter or margarine, cocoa, baking chocolate, and vanilla. Mix in powdered sugar gradually. Add nuts. Press into pan. Cut into 96 pieces (8 by 12). Store in refrigerator.

Nutrition Facts (per serving)

Serving size 1 piece (15g); Servings per recipe 96; Calories 55; Calories from Fat 18; Total Fat 2g (3% DV); Saturated Fat 1g (5% DV); Cholesterol 0; Vitamin A 1% DV; Vitamin C 0; Sodium 8mg (1% DV); Total Carbohydrate 9g (3% DV); Dietary Fiber 1g (4% DV); Protein 1g; Calcium 1% DV; Iron 2% DV

Tonto's Pie

The first ingredient tells you why it is his favorite.

8 SERVINGS

2 cups cooked pinto beans

1/4 to 1/2 cup warm water

1 cup sugar

1/2 teaspoon salt

1 teaspoon cinnamon

1/2 teaspoon ginger

1/4 teaspoon cloves

1/4 teaspoon nutmeg

3 eggs

12-ounce can evaporated skim milk

2 tablespoons water

10-inch unbaked deep-dish pie
  shell, homemade or refrigerated

Light whipped topping and freshly
  grated nutmeg for topping

Use pinto beans that have been cooked until tender. Puree beans and water in a blender or food processor. Scrape down sides occasionally, if needed, and puree until smooth. Preheat oven to 425°. Combine pinto bean puree, sugar, salt, and spices in mixing bowl. Add eggs; mix well. Add evaporated skim milk and water; mix. Pour into pie shell. Bake for 15 minutes. Reduce temperature to 350° and continue baking for an additional 45 minutes, or until knife inserted in center of filling comes out clean. Cool. Garnish with light whipped topping and freshly grated nutmeg.

Nutrition Facts (per serving)

Serving size 1 wedge (160g); Servings per recipe 8; Calories 343; Calories from Fat 90; Total Fat 10g (15% DV); Saturated Fat 3g (15% DV); Cholesterol 104mg (35% DV); Vitamin A 6% DV; Vitamin C 1% DV; Sodium 353mg (15% DV); Total Carbohydrate 53g (18% DV); Dietary Fiber 3g (12% DV); Protein 11g; Calcium 18% DV; Iron 14% DV

Pudding Cake

Is this spicy delight a pudding or a cake? Indulge while it is warm and then decide.

12 SERVINGS

Nonstick vegetable cooking spray

2 1/2 cups applesauce

1 cup sugar

2 teaspoons vanilla flavoring

1 egg, beaten

2 cups mashed pinto beans, warm

1 cup all-purpose flour, sifted

1 teaspoon salt

1 teaspoon allspice

1 teaspoon baking soda

1/2 teaspoon baking powder

1 teaspoon cinnamon

1 cup raisins

Preheat oven to 350°. Lightly spray a 9-inch tube pan and set aside. In a large bowl, mix applesauce and sugar. Add vanilla and egg; beat well. Stir in warm beans. Add dry ingredients and mix well. Stir in raisins. Batter will be stiff. Spoon into pan. Bake for 1 hour. Cool in pan for 15 minutes. Loosen edges of cake with a flat spatula or knife and turn out on plate. Serve warm.

Nutrition Facts (per serving)

Serving size 1 piece (125g); Servings per recipe 12; Calories 210; Calories from Fat 9; Total Fat 1g (1% DV); Saturated Fat 0; Cholesterol 23mg (8% DV); Vitamin A 1% DV; Vitamin C 2% DV; Sodium 270mg (11% DV); Total Carbohydrate 48g (16% DV); Dietary Fiber 4g (16% DV); Protein 5g; Calcium 3% DV; Iron 10% DV

Apple Bean Spice Cake

A golden apple cake that's delicious.

16 SERVINGS

Nonstick vegetable cooking spray	1/2 teaspoon salt
1 cup sugar	1/2 teaspoon cloves
1/4 cup margarine	1/2 teaspoon allspice
2 eggs	2 cups finely chopped peeled apples
2 cups mashed pinto beans, warm	1 cup golden raisins
1 cup all-purpose flour	1/2 cup chopped walnuts
1 teaspoon baking soda	2 teaspoons vanilla flavoring
1 teaspoon cinnamon	Easy Glaze (recipe below)

Preheat oven to 375°. Spray a 10-inch tube pan with cooking spray and lightly dust with flour. Set aside. Cream together the sugar and margarine in a large mixing bowl. Add eggs one at a time and beat well. Add mashed beans and beat well. Sift together the flour, baking soda, and spices; fold into mixture. Fold in apples, golden raisins, nuts, and vanilla. Pour into prepared pan and bake for 45 minutes or until toothpick inserted in center comes out clean. Cool and remove from pan. Glaze and garnish with nuts. Cut into 16 slices.

Easy Glaze

1/2 cup powdered sugar, sifted	1/3 cup chopped nuts
2 teaspoons milk	
1/4 teaspoon vanilla, lemon, almond, or	
rum flavoring	

Mix first three ingredients until smooth. Drizzle on cake, then sprinkle with nuts for garnish.

Nutrition Facts (per serving)

Serving size 1 piece (95g); Servings per recipe 16; Calories 245; Calories from Fat 72; Total Fat 8g (12% DV); Saturated Fat 1g (5% DV); Cholesterol 34mg (11% DV); Vitamin A 3% DV; Vitamin C 2% DV; Sodium 165mg (7% DV); Total Carbohydrate 41g (14%); Dietary Fiber 3g (12% DV); Protein 5g; Calcium 3% DV; Iron 10% DV

Chewy Garbanzo Spice Bars

Sunny, spicy, and sweet.

24 SERVINGS

Nonstick vegetable cooking spray

2 cups cooked garbanzo beans, mashed

1 1/2 cups brown sugar

2 eggs

3/4 cup applesauce

1 1/2 cups warm mashed potatoes

2 teaspoons vanilla flavoring

1 1/2 cups rolled oats

1 cup all-purpose flour

2 teaspoons cinnamon

2 teaspoons baking powder

1 teaspoon baking soda

3/4 cup sunflower kernels, raw or roasted

Preheat oven to 350°. Spray a 9-inch x 13-inch cake pan with cooking spray; set aside. Combine mashed garbanzo beans, brown sugar, eggs, applesauce, potatoes, and vanilla; mix until well blended. Combine dry ingredients. Add to batter and mix well. Stir in sunflower kernels. Pour into prepared pan. Bake for 30 minutes or until no imprint remains when touched lightly. Cut into 24 pieces (6 by 4).

Nutrition Facts (per serving)

Serving size 1 bar (74g); Servings per recipe 24; Calories 175; Calories from Fat 45; Total Fat 5g (8% DV); Saturated Fat 1g (5% DV); Cholesterol 23mg (8% DV); Vitamin A 1% DV; Vitamin C 2% DV; Sodium 115mg (5% DV); Total Carbohydrate 30g (8% DV); Dietary Fiber 2g (8% DV); Protein 5g; Calcium 4% DV; Iron 11% DV

Mario's Cake

A flourless cake with great eye appeal and great taste.

6 SERVINGS

Nonstick vegetable cooking spray

1/2 cup dried garbanzo beans or 1 1/2 cups
   canned garbanzo beans, drained

1/2 cup skim milk

1/3 cup sugar

3 large eggs, separated

1/8 teaspoon salt

1/8 teaspoon nutmeg

1/4 teaspoon cinnamon

1/2 teaspoon vanilla flavoring

1 teaspoon rum extract

Sliced strawberries, kiwi, pineapple,
   or other fresh fruit for garnish

Preheat oven to 350°. Spray the bottom and sides of a 9-inch round cake pan with cooking spray. Cut waxed paper to fit the bottom of the pan. (Use waxed paper even with a Teflon-coated pan, although you may omit spraying the sides.)

Put milk and sugar in a blender or food processor; add the garbanzo beans and blend until smooth. Allow to stand while other ingredients are prepared. Beat the egg whites and salt until stiff but not dry, set aside. (Always beat the egg whites before the yolks because then you don't need to wash the beaters in between. Egg whites must be beaten with very clean, dry beaters.) In a separate, large mixing bowl, beat the yolks until thick. Add the salt, spices, flavorings, and garbanzo beans to the yolks and mix thoroughly. Fold in the egg whites. Pour the batter into the cake pan and bake for 40 minutes or until cake is firm in the center. Cool on a rack for 10 minutes, then remove the cake from the pan and carefully peel off the waxed paper. Cool to room temperature, then cover and refrigerate several hours or overnight before serving. When ready to serve, garnish top with sliced fresh fruit arranged in a circular pattern to cover cake top.

TIP: This cake would be nice for a leisurely brunch on the patio.

Nutrition Facts (per serving)

Serving size 1 slice (122g); Servings per recipe 6; Calories 168; Calories from Fat 36; Total Fat 4g (6% DV); Saturated Fat 1g (5% DV); Cholesterol 137mg (46% DV); Vitamin A 4% DV; Vitamin C 33% DV; Sodium 90mg (4% DV); Total Carbohydrate 26g (9% DV); Dietary Fiber 3g (12% DV); Protein 8g; Calcium 7% DV; Iron 10% DV

Web of Intrigue Dessert

*Tofu creates a reduced-fat dessert with the texture and flavor
of cheesecake. This showy dessert is much easier than you think!*

12 SERVINGS

....

Graham Cracker Crust

1 1/2 cups graham cracker crumbs	*4 tablespoons margarine, melted*
1/4 cup powdered sugar, sifted	

Preheat oven to 300°. Prepare graham cracker crumbs using a blender or food processor or put crackers between two sheets of waxed paper and crush with a rolling pin. Stir powdered sugar and melted margarine into crumbs. Pat firmly across bottom and up sides of 9-inch spring form pan. Strive to have crumbs evenly distributed. Bake for 15 minutes. Remove from oven and cool before filling and baking.

....

Tofu Filling

2 eggs	*1 teaspoon vanilla flavoring*
16 ounces soft tofu, cubed	*4 ounces light cream cheese, cubed*
1/2 cup maple syrup	*Raspberry Sauce (recipe follows)*
2 tablespoons fresh lemon juice	*Web of Intrigue (recipe follows)*
1 tablespoon grated lemon zest	

Preheat oven to 350°. Put eggs, cubed tofu, and syrup in blender or food processor; blend until smooth. Add lemon juice, lemon zest, vanilla, and cream cheese, and blend until smooth. Pour into prepared graham cracker crust. Bake for one hour. To test for doneness, toothpick inserted in center should come out almost clean. Allow cake to sit in oven (turned off) about an hour. Chill at least 12 hours before serving, to allow flavor to develop. If cake shrinks excessively, the baking temperature was too high. Spread top with Raspberry Sauce. Create web on top as described on the next page. Serve in wedges.

Raspberry Sauce

10-ounce package frozen raspberries in syrup, thawed
1/4 teaspoon almond extract

Blend raspberries and extract in a blender or food processor until smooth. If desired, press through a fine sieve to remove seeds.

Web of Intrigue

1/2 cup tofu   *1 tablespoon honey*

Blend tofu and honey together using a blender, food processor, or electric mixer. Spoon mixture into a pastry bag with a writing tip. Make concentric, graduated circles on top of raspberry sauce. Using a skewer or toothpick, pull from center to edge of cake and then back to center. Continue until you have created a web on cake top.

Nutrition Facts (per serving)

Serving size 1 wedge (120g); Servings per recipe 12; Calories 222; Calories from Fat 81; Total Fat 9g (14% DV); Saturated Fat 3g (15% DV); Cholesterol 51mg (17% DV); Vitamin A 6% DV; Vitamin C 8%; Sodium 144mg (6% DV); Total Carbohydrate 30g 10% (DV); Dietary Fiber 1g (4% DV); Protein 6g; Calcium 6% DV; Iron 9% DV

Raspberry Tofu Dessert

A delicious low-cal dessert.

6 SERVINGS

10-ounce package frozen raspberries,
    partially thawed

8 ounces soft tofu

1 teaspoon vanilla extract

1 cup low-fat whipped topping,
    thawed

2 tablespoons sugar, if desired

Put raspberries and tofu in blender or food processor and blend until smooth. Fold in remaining ingredients. Pour into a flat pan and allow to freeze. Stir occasionally to avoid ice crystals. If desired, serve garnished with a mint leaf or a few fresh berries.

Nutrition Facts (per serving)

Serving size 1/2 cup (98g); Servings per recipe 6; Calories 115; Calories from Fat 27; Total Fat 3g (5% DV); Saturated Fat 2g (10% DV); Cholesterol 0; Vitamin A 2% DV; Vitamin C 13% DV; Sodium 5mg (1% DV); Total Carbohydrate 19g (6% DV); Dietary Fiber 1g (4% DV); Protein 3g; Calcium 4% DV; Iron 6% DV

Chocolate Swirl Pie

Extra smooth, extra flavor.

8 SERVINGS

8 to 10 ounces firm tofu, cubed   *2 eggs*

1/2 cup honey   *9-inch graham cracker crust*

1 1/2 teaspoons vanilla flavoring   *1/2 cup semisweet chocolate pieces*

Preheat oven to 325°. Blend tofu with honey using an electric mixer at medium speed until thoroughly combined. Add vanilla and eggs and beat until well blended. Pour into graham cracker crust. Melt chocolate pieces in small saucepan over low heat. Drop melted chocolate by teaspoonfuls over pie. Swirl chocolate through creamy tofu mixture using a knife or fork. Bake 20 to 25 minutes, or until center appears set. Cool on rack. Cover and chill in refrigerator.

TIP: Short on time? Microwave it! Prepare creamy tofu as above and pour into crust. Put chocolate pieces in small glass bowl and cover with waxed paper. Cook on high for 1 1/2 minutes to melt. Add to pie as directed above. Cook pie in microwave on high for 5 minutes or until center appears set. If the oven doesn't have a turntable, rotate pie a quarter turn after every minute. Cool on rack. Cover and chill in refrigerator.

Nutrition Facts (per serving)

Serving size 1 slice (105g); Servings per recipe 8; Calories 280; Calories from Fat 99; Total Fat 11g (17% DV); Saturated Fat 3g (15% DV); Cholesterol 69mg (23% DV); Vitamin A 6% DV; Vitamin C 0; Sodium 220mg (9% DV); Total Carbohydrate 42g (14% DV); Dietary Fiber 2g (8% DV); Protein 6g; Calcium 5% DV; Iron 9% DV

Pumpkin Tofu Pie

Low fat and low sugar, with excellent flavor!

8 SERVINGS

*9-inch deep-dish pie crust, homemade,
   frozen, or refrigerated
1 cup soft tofu, or 10.5-ounce package
1 1/2 cups cooked pumpkin
1/2 cup sugar*

*2 tablespoons cornstarch
1/2 cup skim milk
2 to 3 teaspoons pumpkin pie spice
1/2 teaspoon salt*

Preheat oven to 400°. Prepare and pre-bake crust for 5 to 7 minutes. Remove from oven and cool. Reduce oven temperature to 350°. Combine all remaining ingredients in a blender or food processor and blend until very smooth. Pour into pre-baked pie shell. Bake one hour, or until knife blade inserted in center comes out almost clean. Cool on a rack and serve at room temperature. Refrigerate remaining pie.

Nutrition Facts (per serving)

Serving size 1 slice (130g); Servings per recipe 8; Calories 210; Calories from Fat 81; Total Fat 9g (14% DV); Saturated Fat 2g (10% DV); Cholesterol 0; Vitamin A 203% DV; Vitamin C 4% DV; Sodium 284mg (12% DV); Total Carbohydrate 30g (10% DV); Dietary Fiber 2g (8% DV); Protein 5g; Calcium 7% DV; Iron 12% DV

Beets

HISTORY

Wild beets, growing along the shores of the Mediterranean, were used in ancient
times only for their greens. Greeks of the 5th century considered the greens indi-
gestible and fit only for the poorest of the poor. And no one at all ate the root.
Once the sweet and gentle flavor of the beet root was discovered, it became a popular food with a medicinal bonus. It was used to heal bones. The juice of the
pounded root was recommended for wounds caused by animal bites. By the Middle Ages the beet was eaten and enjoyed by peoples from the Baltic Sea to the
Aegean Sea. Garlic lovers ate roasted beets to remove the garlic odor from their
breath.

Beets aren't just red. Yellow beets are considered sweeter than the red and are
sometimes crushed with apples in a press to give a richer, golden color to the
cider. Chard is a white beet, bred over the centuries to minimize the root and
enlarge the stalk and luxuriant leaves.s

SEASON

June through October are the months of peak supply for fresh beets. The rest of
the year you may see fresh beets in the supermarket, but they have been held in
cold storage and their sugar content has decreased.

QUALITY AND STORAGE

Small, young beets are the most tender. Late in the season, beets are larger, less tender, and may have woody cores. Choose smooth, firm, round beets with a deep color. Avoid beets with soft spots or shriveled skin.

The beet is one vegetable that retains nearly all the quality of freshness when canned. The flavor and texture of canned beets are excellent.

Store fresh beets in the refrigerator. Cut tops off to within an inch of the bulb. Don't cut into the bulb, for the beet will begin to bleed. To maintain moisture, place the unwashed roots in a plastic bag. Beets will keep in the refrigerator for up to three weeks.

NUTRITIONAL QUALITY

We remember our mothers telling us that beets were good for building blood. Although beets are not particularly rich in iron, they are one of the best sources of folate, which is necessary for making red blood cells. One half cup of cooked beets provides 4% of the Daily Value for iron, 2% of the Daily Value for zinc, 8% of the Daily Value for vitamin C, 3% of the Daily Value for dietary fiber, and 18% of the Daily Value for folate.

Orange Drop Cookies

These delicately flavored morsels have a surprising ingredient.

3 DOZEN

Nonstick vegetable cooking spray	*1 cup brown sugar, firmly packed*
2 cups all-purpose flour	*3/4 cup vegetable oil*
1/2 teaspoon baking soda	*2 cups oatmeal, regular or quick*
3/4 teaspoon salt	*cooking*
1 1/2 teaspoons cinnamon	*1/2 cup walnuts, chopped*
1/4 teaspoon cloves	*2 teaspoons grated orange rind*
1/4 teaspoon nutmeg	*(1 orange)*
2 eggs	*1 cup beet puree**

Preheat oven to 375°. Spray cookie sheets with cooking spray and set aside. Sift flour, soda, salt, and spices together; set aside. Combine eggs, brown sugar, and oil in mixing bowl. Beat thoroughly. Add sifted dry ingredients, oats, walnuts, orange rind, and beet puree. Blend thoroughly but don't overmix. Drop rounded teaspoonfuls of dough onto prepared cookie sheets about 2 inches apart. Bake for 12 to 15 minutes.

*TIP: Babyfood is a quick source of beet puree. You can also quickly make your own using canned sliced or diced beets in a blender or food processor.

Nutrition Facts (per serving)

Serving size 1 cookie (33g); Servings per recipe 36; Calories 123; Calories from Fat 54; Total Fat 6g (9% DV); Saturated Fat 1g (5% DV); Cholesterol 15mg (5% DV); Vitamin A 0; Vitamin C 1% DV; Sodium 66mg (3% DV); Total Carbohydrate 15g (5% DV); Dietary Fiber 1g (4% DV); Protein 2g; Calcium 1% DV; Iron 5% DV

Mystery Pie

A relative of the shoofly pie.

8 SERVINGS

3/4 cup all-purpose flour	1 egg, beaten
1/2 cup sugar	3/4 cup evaporated skim milk
1/4 teaspoon salt	1/2 teaspoon almond extract
1/2 teaspoon cinnamon	2 cups beet puree*
2 tablespoons solid shortening	9-inch unbaked deep-dish pastry
1/3 cup light molasses	shell, homemade, frozen, or
1 1/2 teaspoons baking soda	refrigerated

Preheat oven to 400°. Combine flour, sugar, salt, and cinnamon with shortening, and mix until it resembles coarse crumbs. In another bowl, combine molasses and soda. Stir in the egg, evaporated milk, flavoring, and puree. Pour half the liquid mixture into pie shell, add 1/4 of the crumbs and stir. Pour in the remaining liquid mixture and top with remainder of the crumbs. This time do not stir. Bake 12 minutes until crust starts to brown. Reduce oven temperature to 325° and bake for 45 minutes, until pie is firm.

*TIP: Baby food is a quick source of beet puree. Or make your own using canned sliced or diced beets in a blender or food processor.

Nutrition Facts (per serving)

Serving size 1 wedge (150g); Servings per recipe 8; Calories 280; Calories from Fat 99; Total Fat 11g (17% DV); Saturated Fat 3g (15% DV); Cholesterol 35mg (12% DV); Vitamin A 5% DV; Vitamin C 5% DV; Sodium 610mg (25% DV); Total Carbohydrate 39g (13% DV); Dietary Fiber 3g (12% DV); Protein 6g; Calcium 18% DV; Iron 31% DV

Cabbage

HISTORY

Once upon a time in China, a kindly but very poor man lived on a popular mountain trail. Yung-po always offered travelers a place to rest and a cool drink of water from his well. He wanted to offer food but rarely had any even for himself. One day a traveler thanked him by leaving a small package of cabbage seeds. "Plant these behind your hut," said the traveler, "and you shall find a most excellent wife and you will have enough jade to keep you and your family in comfort for the rest of your life."

Yung-po planted the seeds behind his house and when the plants were ankle-high he met a young woman with whom he fell in love. When he asked her to be his wife, she replied, "I will marry you when you are rich enough to give me two bracelets of white jade."

Sadly, Yung-po returned home. Lonely and discouraged, he decided to work in his cabbage field. At least the cabbages were growing as fine and green as jade. Suddenly the hoe struck something hard. Digging carefully he uncovered an earthen jar containing five white jade bracelets and many other rich ornaments.

The kindly traveler had buried them there many years before. When he had returned to recover them, he was touched by the kindness and generosity of poverty-stricken Yung-po. The traveler had decided to leave the rich treasure for the poor man, using the cabbage seeds as a tactful way to present the gift.

Cabbage was highly regarded by the ancients. It was said to be Roman general Pompey's favorite dish. It was highly celebrated by ancient physicians as the cure for all ills. Eaten after a meal, it was thought to aid digestion. The Romans also used cabbage as a cure for melancholy and as a poultice for sores and carbuncles.

During the Middle Ages one medical theory was the "Doctrine of Signatures." According to this belief, ailments should be treated with something in nature that looked like the afflicted body part. Cabbage fit nicely into the theory. Because cabbage forms a head, it was clear that cabbage was good for ailments of the head, such as drunkenness and headache.

The Roman statesman Cato advised eating it raw or pickled before a meal to counteract the effects of alcohol. Greek peasants agreed that a little cabbage could prevent intoxication from drinking wine. Here is the story they tell to explain why.

A haughty Grecian prince was inordinately proud of his vineyard. No one had vines as lush or grapes so large and sweet. No one, that is, except his neighbor, whose vines were small and scraggly but whose grapes were even larger and more beautiful than the prince's. Day by day the prince's envy grew until one night he disguised himself and crept into the neighbor's vineyard. Silently he proceeded to destroy each vine. Just as he was destroying the last plant, he was caught and taken before a judge for justice. Since there was no question of his guilt, the court decreed that he should be punished by being chained to one of his own grapevines near the highway where all could see his shame. The prince was so humiliated that great tears began to roll down his cheeks. As the tears touched the ground they turned into cabbages. This was the origin of cabbage and the explanation for the antagonism between cabbage and grapes.

For centuries cabbage has been credited with extraordinary virtues—an antidote for poison, a cure for dog and snake bites, sniffed into the nostrils as a purge for the brain, a treatment for sore throat and cough, a way to improve poor eyesight, and a cure for tremor. Cabbage leaves laid on the head would prevent baldness. But cabbage had a downside, too. If eaten at the wrong time, it could cause nightmares.

Our word for this mildest of cruciferous vegetables comes from Latin where the common people called cabbage "caput," meaning head. In France this was transformed into "cabus" and then "cabache," which English speakers mispronounced "cabbage." Cole and colewort are old names for cabbage. The small round head of the cabbage plant is sometimes called the cabbage heart or the cabbage apple.

Sauerkraut is pickled cabbage. Although we associate it with Germanic, Baltic and Slavic countries, sauerkraut's roots are in the Far East. Builders of the Great Wall of China ate sauerkraut long before most European nations were formed.

Before vitamin C was discovered, sauerkraut kept northern peoples scurvy-free during the long winters. Captain James Cook is said to have carried it on sea voyages to keep his crew healthy.

The sauerkrauts popular in the United States have a sour flavor. But in eastern European markets, sauerkraut is readily available in at least three flavors: sour, sweet-sour, and sweet.

SEASON

Cabbage is available all year at reasonable prices. Adaptable to a variety of conditions, it can be grown nearly everywhere in North America. During the winter months the supply comes from Texas, California, and Florida. Savoy cabbage is usually available only September through March.

QUALITY AND STORAGE

There are many kinds of cabbage: round headed and cone headed, compact headed and loose headed, smooth leaved and wrinkled leaved, green and red. The crisp, smooth-leaved variety is the most common. Crinkled-leaved cabbage, known as savoy, has a milder flavor, and is less brittle.

Cabbage heads should be firm and heavy for their size, with compact, pale green or deep red leaves. Outer leaves should look fresh and be reasonably free from blemishes. Avoid a cabbage with separate leaves growing from the main stem below the head. These cabbages usually have a stronger flavor.

Store fresh, unwashed cabbage in a plastic bag in the vegetable bin of the refrigerator. Uncut cabbage will maintain good quality for 2 weeks. Once cabbage is cut, the edges will discolor. To delay this oxidation, keep cut edges tightly covered with plastic wrap. Rubbing the cut surface with lemon juice will also help prevent darkening.

Sauerkraut can be purchased canned, refrigerated, or fresh. Jars of refrigerated kraut will keep well for a week. Fresh sauerkraut, in loose bags in the produce bins, should be refrigerated at home and used within a week.

NUTRITIONAL QUALITY

Cabbage is a terrific nutritional bargain: fat free, low in calories, and a good source of dietary fiber. One cup of shredded cabbage has only 16 calories. Like other vegetables, cabbage is a good source of potassium. In addition, one cup of raw cabbage gives you 55% of the Daily Value for vitamin C and 20% of the Daily Value for folate. Red cabbage has more vitamin C than green cabbage. Savoy cabbage has a significant amount of beta-carotene, although red and green cabbages do not. Sauerkraut has one nutritional drawback—it is very high in sodium. Before using sauerkraut, rinse in cool running water to reduce its sodium content.

Cabbage has additional health benefits as a member of the family of cruciferous vegetables. Research is showing that these vegetables have anti-cancer properties. In laboratory experiments, animals fed cruciferous vegetables develop fewer tumors. In the real world, people who eat generous amounts of vegetables are less likely to die of lung cancer. Although the exact component or combination of components of cabbage or other cruciferous vegetables that reduces risk for cancer is not known, recent research has focused on the indoles. These nitrogen-containing compounds have been isolated from cabbage and fed to laboratory animals. The animals who received a daily dose of indoles equal to eating half a head of cabbage a day were protected from estrogen-induced cancers such as breast cancer. Unfortunately, scientists are still a long way from showing that eating cabbage and other cruciferous vegetables guarantees freedom from cancer. In the meantime, generous consumption of these vegetables will provide you important nutrients, add interesting flavors to your meals, and just may reduce your risk for some types of cancers.

Kraut Crisps

A thin, crunchy cookie you will love.

6 DOZEN

1 1/4 cups (14-ounce can) sauerkraut	2 1/2 cups all-purpose flour
1 cup margarine	1 teaspoon baking soda
1 cup brown sugar	1/2 teaspoon salt
1 cup granulated sugar	3 cups oatmeal
1 egg, beaten	Nonstick vegetable cooking spray
1 teaspoon vanilla	

Rinse sauerkraut, drain well, cut through with a sharp knife; set aside. Cream margarine and sugars. Add egg and vanilla; beat well. Stir drained sauerkraut into mixture. Add dry ingredients. Form into 2 or 3 long rolls and wrap in waxed paper. Chill 12 hours or several days. (They can be frozen and baked later.)

Preheat oven to 375°. Slice rolls into 1/4-inch slices with a sharp knife. The thinness of the slices influences the crispness of the cookie. Bake on a lightly sprayed baking sheet about 10 to 12 minutes, or until lightly browned.

Nutrition Facts (per serving)

Serving size 1 cookie (20g); Servings per recipe 72; Calories 73; Calories from Fat 18; Total Fat 2g (3% DV); Saturated Fat 1g (4% DV); Cholesterol 7mg (2% DV); Vitamin A 2% DV; Vitamin C 1% DV; Sodium 97mg (4% DV); Total Carbohydrate 11g (4% DV); Dietary Fiber 1g (4% DV); Protein 1g; Calcium 1% DV; Iron 2% DV

Rosy Cranberry Pie

Pretty, tasty, and fiber rich. A dynamite combination!

8 SERVINGS

9-inch unbaked pie shell, plus pastry strips   1/4 teaspoon salt
  for top, homemade or refrigerated   1 1/4 cups cold water
1 tablespoon margarine, melted   2 cups finely shredded cabbage
2 tablespoons cornstarch   2 cups cranberries
1 1/4 cups sugar   1/8 teaspoon almond extract

Preheat oven to 425°. Brush unbaked pie shell with about 2 teaspoons of margarine. Reserve any unused dough for strips or cutouts for top of pie. Blend cornstarch with sugar and salt. Add water slowly, mix until smooth, and cook until mixture thickens, stirring constantly. Add the cabbage, cranberries, 1 teaspoon margarine and all that remains from brushing pastry crust. Cook 5 minutes. Stir in almond extract. Place filling in unbaked pie shell. Cover top with 1/2-inch strips, sealing strips securely to shell. Bake for 20 minutes, or until pastry is brown and filling is bubbling.

Nutrition Facts (per serving)

Serving size 1 slice (195g); Servings per recipe 8; Calories 340; Calories from Fat 117; Total Fat 13g (20% DV); Saturated Fat 3g (15% DV); Cholesterol 0; Vitamin A 2% DV; Vitamin C 19% DV; Sodium 410mg (17% DV); Total Carbohydrate 54g (18% DV); Dietary Fiber 2g (8% DV); Protein 3g; Calcium 3% DV; Iron 8% DV

Chocolate Surprise Cake

They won't ask what's in it. They'll just declare it the best chocolate cake ever.

16 SERVINGS

Nonstick vegetable cooking spray

8-ounce can sauerkraut, drained, rinsed

1/2 cup margarine

1 1/2 cups sugar

3 eggs

1 teaspoon vanilla flavoring

1 cup mashed potatoes

1 1/2 cups all-purpose flour

1 teaspoon baking soda

1 teaspoon baking powder

1/4 teaspoon salt

2/3 cup cocoa

1 cup water

Creamy Chocolate Frosting

(recipe below)

Preheat oven to 350°. Spray a 9-inch x 13-inch pan with cooking spray; set aside. Chop or snip drained sauerkraut; set aside. Cream margarine and sugar until light and fluffy. Add eggs one at a time, beating after each addition. Stir in vanilla flavoring and mashed potatoes. Sift dry ingredients together, and add to creamed mixture alternately with water. Fold in sauerkraut. Pour batter into prepared pan and bake for 45 to 50 minutes. Cool. Frost with Creamy Chocolate Frosting. Cut into 16 pieces (4 by 4).

Creamy Chocolate Frosting

6 ounces chocolate chips

4 tablespoons margarine

1/2 cup yogurt cheese (page XX)

1 teaspoon vanilla extract

1/4 teaspoon salt

2½ to 2¾ cups powdered sugar

Melt chocolate chips and margarine over low heat or in microwave. Stir in yogurt cheese, vanilla, and salt. Gradually add powdered sugar, mixing well after each addition, until it reaches a spreadable consistency. Beat until smooth.

Nutrition Facts (per serving)

Serving size 1 piece (123g); Servings per recipe 16; Calories 350; Calories from Fat 125; Total Fat 14g (22% DV); Saturated Fat 5g (25% DV); Cholesterol 52mg (17% DV); Vitamin A 8% DV; Vitamin C 5% DV; Sodium 400mg (17% DV); Total Carbohydrate 56g (19% DV); Dietary Fiber 3g (12% DV); Protein 5g; Calcium 6% DV; Iron 10% DV

Carrots

HISTORY

Carrots are traditional foods of northern peoples because the best carrots grow in cool climates. The ancient Romans learned of carrots only when they conquered Gaul. The Dutch were among the first to raise carrots to popular status, although carrots were also an important food among the native Americans of the southwest United States.

Like many other vegetables, carrots had their folk medicine uses. If you were plagued by the devil, a drink of carrot juice would protect you. If your sanity was in danger, a beverage made of carrots and other ingredients would restore your reason. Carrot oil is said to be a moth repellent.

In ancient England women who couldn't afford exotic feathers used the feathery carrot tops to decorate their hair, hats, and dresses for holidays. The carrot is cousin to Queen Anne's Lace, the delicate, white, umbrella-like wild flower familiar along North American roadsides. Queen Anne's Lace is sometimes called wild carrot, but the root is woody and inedible.

Carrots come in colors ranging from near white to yellow to orange and near red. The darker the color, the more nutritious. Some varieties of carrots grow a foot and a half long.

SEASON

Fresh carrots are available at inexpensive prices all year long. In the winter they are shipped from fields in California. In the spring, summer, and fall, they are available from local farmers' markets.

QUALITY AND STORAGE

Look for carrots with bright, deep orange color. Don't be misled by the orange plastic bags in which carrots are sometimes packaged. Try to see the color of the carrots themselves. Look for straight carrots and avoid those that are gnarled. Crooked carrots are often woody and tough (and hard to peel!). Watch out for carrots that have started to produce tiny white rootlets. This is a sign of old age. Avoid carrots that are wilted, flabby, shriveled, or cracked. Although carrots are generally more succulent when young and small, large, mature carrots can be even sweeter as well as have a fine, dense texture.

To preserve moisture, keep carrots in a plastic bag in the refrigerator. If you harvest your own carrots or buy carrots with the green tops still on, remove the greens by twisting or cutting, but don't cut into the carrot itself. Pretty though they may be, the feathery carrot tops draw water out of the carrot flesh, greatly decreasing its quality. Carrots store well and will maintain quality for 2 weeks or more in the refrigerator.

NUTRITIONAL QUALITY

Carrots are one of the richest sources of beta-carotene. In fact, as you may have guessed, this plant form of vitamin A was named for carrots, where it was first discovered. Pure beta-carotene is deep orange and is what gives carrots their appealing color. All fruits and vegetables that are deep yellow or orange are rich in beta-carotene. Beta-carotene is even used as an additive in processed foods to give them a golden color.

One carrot has only 42 calories but 200% of the Daily Value for vitamin A, 16% of the Daily Value for dietary fiber, and modest amounts of vitamin C and iron. A research study found that people who ate 7 ounces (about three medium) of carrots every day had an average 11% drop in their blood cholesterol. Of course, the effect may have been due not to the carrots themselves, but to the fact that eating so many carrots displaced fatty foods from their daily menus.

Many research studies have shown that eating carrots (and other carotene-rich vegetables) lowers the risk for several types of cancer. The evidence is strong, but again it's not certain if it's the beta-carotene that is the effective agent, or the dietary fiber, or some combination of the many components that make up vegetables. What is certain is that vegetables are very, very good for you. And carrots are one of the superstar vegetables.

Did your mother tell you to eat your carrots because they are good for your eyes? Well, she was right. The beta-carotene in carrots is converted to vitamin A in your body. In the retina of the eye, vitamin A is an indispensable part of the apparatus that transmits light signals to the brain, thus permitting you to see. Carrots won't improve near-sightedness or other visual problems that require glasses, but they will help you see in the dark. Vitamin A deficiency can result in total loss of vision. Millions of children in developing countries are permanently blinded because they didn't get vitamin A in their foods.

Can you eat too many carrots? Only if you eat so many you fail to eat other nutritious foods. Eating lots of carrots can turn your skin orange. All that beta-carotene gets stored in your skin. It's not dangerous, you'll just be a funny color.

For another dessert using carrots, see Confetti Cookies, page 54.

Carrot Raisin Bars

The preteens will love to bake and eat these bars.

12 SERVINGS

Nonstick vegetable cooking spray

1/3 cup sugar

1/3 cup margarine

1 egg

1 teaspoon vanilla flavoring

1/4 cup water

3/4 cup all-purpose flour

1 teaspoon baking powder

3/4 teaspoon cinnamon

1/4 teaspoon salt

1/2 cup quick-cooking oats

1/4 cup raisins, chopped

1/2 cup shredded carrot

Preheat oven to 350°. Spray an 8-inch square baking pan with cooking spray; set aside. Beat sugar and margarine with an electric mixer at medium speed until well blended, about 2 minutes. Add egg and vanilla; beat well. Mix in water. Stir together flour, baking powder, cinnamon, and salt. Add to egg mixture, and mix until blended. Stir in oats, raisins, and carrot. Spread dough in pan. Bake for 25 minutes or until toothpick inserted into center comes out clean. Cut into 12 bars (3 by 4).

TO BAKE IN MICROWAVE: Use an 8-inch round ceramic or glass dish. Bake at 30% power for 6 minutes. Give dish one quarter turn. Continue baking on high power for 3 1/2 minutes. Give dish another quarter turn. Test with toothpick for doneness.

Nutrition Facts (per serving)

Serving size 1 bar (35g); Servings per recipe 12; Calories 125; Calories from Fat 54; Total Fat 6g (9% DV); Saturated Fat 1g (5% DV); Cholesterol 23mg (8% DV); Vitamin A 30% DV; Vitamin C 1% DV; Sodium 140mg (6% DV); Total Carbohydrate 17g (6% DV); Dietary Fiber 1g (4% DV); Protein 2g; Calcium 2% DV; Iron 4% DV

Three-Fruit Carrot Bars

Rich with fruits, these easy bars use canned carrots as a handy time saver.

9 DOZEN

Nonstick vegetable cooking spray

16-ounce can carrots, drained

4 eggs

1 1/2 cups sugar

3/4 cup oil

2 teaspoons cinnamon

2 cups flour

2 teaspoons baking soda

1 tablespoon orange juice concentrate

1/4 cup chopped nuts

1/4 cup crushed pineapple, drained

1/4 cup chopped raisins

Orange Icing (recipe follows)

Preheat oven to 350°. Spray an 11-inch x 15-inch pan with cooking spray and set aside. In a food processor or blender, puree the carrots. In a large mixing bowl blend together the carrot puree, eggs, sugar, oil, cinnamon, flour, soda, and orange juice concentrate until evenly mixed. Stir in nuts, pineapple, and raisins. Spread batter in prepared pan. Bake for 25 to 30 minutes or until toothpick inserted in center comes out clean. Frost with Orange Icing. Cut into 9 dozen bars (9 by 12).

Orange Icing

1 tablespoon margarine

1 teaspoon vanilla extract

2 cups powdered sugar, sifted

1 to 2 tablespoons orange juice

In a medium-sized mixing bowl blend margarine and vanilla extract. Add powdered sugar and 1 tablespoon orange juice. Beat until smooth. Add more orange juice if needed to get spreading consistency.

Nutrition Facts (per serving)

Serving size 1 bar (16g); Servings per recipe 108; Calories 48; Calories from Fat 18; Total Fat 2g (3% DV); Saturated Fat 0; Cholesterol 10mg (3% DV); Vitamin A 8% DV; Vitamin C 1% DV; Sodium 26mg (1% DV); Total Carbohydrate 7g (2% DV); Dietary Fiber 0; Protein 1g; Calcium 0; Iron 1% DV

Danish Carrot Pudding

For years we have served this as the grand finale for Christmas dinner, flaming it dramatically at the table. No one suspects that this rich holiday tradition is chock full of vegetables.

12 SERVINGS

1/2 cup stick margarine	1 teaspoon cloves
1 cup sugar	1 cup chopped nuts
1 cup grated carrots	1 cup grated potatoes, mixed with
1 cup raisins	1 teaspoon baking soda
1 teaspoon cinnamon	1 cup whole wheat flour
1 teaspoon nutmeg	Lemon Sauce (recipe follows)

Cream margarine and sugar until light and fluffy. Stir in remaining ingredients. Pour into oiled 1 1/2-quart pudding mold and cover tightly with lid or aluminum foil. Set on rack in a large kettle, being certain that the mold is stable and doesn't touch the sides of the kettle. (A canning rack will sometimes meet this need, or a crimped ring of aluminum foil can suffice.) Add boiling water to the kettle until the water is three-quarters of the way up the side of the mold. Put a tight fitting lid on the kettle and steam for 3 hours over low heat. Add water if necessary to keep water level constant.

To test for doneness, remove the mold's cover and lightly press the center of the pudding. The pudding should be firm and springy. If not, recover as before and steam until the top tests done. When cooking time is completed, invert the pudding onto a plate and cover with plastic wrap until ready to serve. Pudding can be prepared 3 to 4 days in advance, refrigerated, and then warmed in the microwave on high power for 2 to 3 minutes. To flame the pudding, lightly warm a small amount of lemon extract, rum, or brandy (1 to 2 tablespoons). Working quickly, pour the warmed alcohol over the pudding and ignite with a match. Serve with Lemon Sauce.

Lemon Sauce

1 cup sugar

1 tablespoon cornstarch

1 egg, beaten

1 cup boiling water

Juice of one lemon

Grated rind of one lemon

1 tablespoon butter or margarine

In a small saucepan, mix together sugar, cornstarch, and egg until smooth. Add boiling water, then bring to boil again, stirring constantly. Remove from heat; stir in juice and grated rind. Add butter or margarine and stir until melted. Serve warm. Makes about 2 cups.

Nutrition Facts (per serving)

Serving size 1/2 cup (100g); Servings per recipe 12; Calories 298; Calories from Fat 125; Total Fat 14g (22% DV); Saturated Fat 2g (10% DV); Cholesterol 0; Vitamin A 58% DV; Vitamin C 7% DV; Sodium 166g (7% DV); Total Carbohydrate 43g (14% DV); Dietary Fiber 3g (12% DV); Protein 4g; Calcium 3% DV; Iron 6% DV

New Carrot Cake

An old favorite with a new twist you'll love!

16 SERVINGS

Nonstick vegetable cooking spray
1 cup all-purpose flour
1 cup whole wheat flour
1/2 cup wheat germ
2 teaspoons baking soda
1/2 teaspoon salt
2 teaspoons cinnamon

3/4 cup vegetable oil
2 cups sugar
2 eggs
3 cups finely grated carrots
Light Cream Cheese Frosting
(recipe follows)

Preheat oven to 350°. Spray and flour two 9-inch round cake pans.* Set aside. Stir together the next six ingredients; set aside. In large bowl, use an electric mixer to combine oil and sugar. Add eggs one at a time and mix thoroughly. Stir in dry ingredients until batter is uniform. Fold in carrots. Bake 25 to 30 minutes or until toothpick inserted in center comes out clean. Cool on rack. Frost with Light Cream Cheese Frosting.

*This cake fits equally well into a 10-inch tube pan or a 9-inch x 13-inch baking pan. Bake 60 minutes.

Light Cream Cheese Frosting

1 1/2 cups powdered sugar, sifted
8-ounce tub light cream cheese, softened
2 teaspoons vanilla extract

Milk, if needed
1/4 cup wheat germ

Combine powdered sugar and cream cheese until thoroughly blended. Stir in vanilla. (If frosting is too thick, add milk one tablespoon at a time.) Fold wheat germ into frosting. Frost cake. Refrigerate cake. To create a different look, reserve wheat germ and sprinkle onto top and sides after cake is frosted.

Nutrition Facts (per serving)

Serving size 1 piece (100g); Servings per recipe 16; Calories 345; Calories from Fat 125; Total Fat 14g (22% DV); Saturated Fat 3g (15% DV); Cholesterol 42mg (14% DV); Vitamin A 125% DV; Vitamin C 10% DV; Sodium 273mg (11% DV); Total Carbohydrate 53g (18% DV); Dietary Fiber 2g (8% DV); Protein 5g; Calcium 3% DV; Iron 12% DV

Upside-Down Carrot Cake

Combines two American classics to make a new favorite.

12 SERVINGS

20-ounce can pineapple slices, canned in juice

1/2 cup margarine, divided

1/2 cup brown sugar, packed

1/2 cup raisins

3/4 cup granulated white sugar

2 eggs

1 teaspoon vanilla flavoring

1 cup shredded carrots

1 cup all-purpose flour

1/2 cup whole-wheat flour

1/2 teaspoon baking powder

1/2 teaspoon baking soda

1/2 teaspoon cinnamon

1/4 teaspoon ground ginger

1/2 teaspoon salt

1/2 cup chopped almonds

Preheat oven to 350°. Drain pineapple, reserving 1/2 cup liquid. Melt 1/4 cup margarine in 10-inch cast iron skillet or other oven-safe baking pan. Blend in brown sugar. Arrange pineapple over sugar mixture and top with raisins. Cream remaining 1/4 cup margarine with granulated white sugar until light and fluffy. Beat in eggs and vanilla flavoring, and fold in carrots. In a separate bowl combine dry ingredients and almonds. Alternate adding flour mixture and reserved pineapple liquid to creamed mixture, mixing well after each addition. Pour batter over pineapple. Bake for 40 to 45 minutes or until toothpick inserted in center comes out clean. Allow to stand 5 minutes, then invert pan on serving plate. Cut into 12 wedges and serve.

Nutrition Facts (per serving)

Serving size 1 wedge (125g); Servings per recipe 12; Calories 300; Calories from Fat 108; Total Fat 12g (18% DV); Saturated Fat 2g (10% DV); Cholesterol 45mg (15% DV); Vitamin A 59% DV; Vitamin C 10% DV; Sodium 245mg (10% DV); Total Carbohydrate 47g (16% DV); Dietary Fiber 3g (12% DV); Protein 4g; Calcium 5% DV; Iron 9% DV

Celery

HISTORY

Celery, a relative of parsnips, parsley, and carrots, was slow to gain acceptance in the kitchen. Wild celery, growing in salt marshes along the sea coasts, is very bitter. Ancient Romans transplanted it to their gardens and with domestication, the flavor of celery improved. Our word celery comes from the Latin word, selinum, which means "soothing oneself."

In the Middle Ages, celery, like so many of today's popular vegetables, was used mainly for medicinal purposes. It was used as a laxative and a diuretic and to treat gallstones, soothe swellings, and treat wild animals bites—a very versatile remedy. By the mid 1600s it had become popular in English kitchen gardens, where it was grown for use in fresh salads, tossed with oil, vinegar, salt, and pepper.

The leaves and stalks were carried on sea voyages by Captain Cook, one of the few captains who had wisdom beyond the scientific knowledge of his day. The modest amount of vitamin C in celery was enough to make the difference between survival or death from scurvy.

Celery is naturally green, bright green, in fact. North Americans generally prefer the taste and texture of the pale green supermarket celery, which has been blanched. As stalks grow, dirt is mounded around them, shutting out light and preventing development of color.

SEASON

There is an excellent supply of celery available all year. Although a small amount of celery is grown in Canada, Michigan, New York, and Texas, over 90 percent of the celery in our stores comes from California and Florida.

QUALITY AND STORAGE

The darker green the stalks, the more nutrients. On the other hand, the darker stalks tend to be stringier and tougher. Choose bunches that are well-shaped and compact, with fresh, unwilted leaves. The stalks should be so rigid and crisp they feel like they would snap if bent. Avoid flaccid bunches that have lost moisture. Leaves should be light to medium green. The deeper the color, the more intense the flavor. Most people prefer the flavor of celery that is light green. The insides of the ribs should be smooth.

Store celery in a plastic bag in the refrigerator. If the bag is shorter than the stalks, use a larger bag or trim the ends so the bag can be tightly closed to retain celery's natural moisture. Celery is a tender vegetable that can freeze easily. Keep it away from the coldest parts of the refrigerator and away from the inner walls where it can get frozen. Frozen celery can be thawed and used safely, but the texture will never again be crisp and crunchy. Celery will maintain good quality for 1 to 2 weeks in the refrigerator.

NUTRITIONAL QUALITY

Celery is nearly calorie-free because it is largely water. One stalk has only 8 calories. Being mostly water, celery isn't rich in other nutrients. One stalk provides 8% of the Daily Value for vitamin C and only 2% of the Daily Value for vitamin A. Celery is rich in dietary fiber, though; one stalk provides 2 of the 25 grams recommended daily.

Some people think celery is high in salt and can't be eaten by people who are watching their sodium intake. It's true that celery has more sodium per ounce than many other vegetables, but the total amount of sodium is still very small compared to processed foods. One stalk has only 63 grams of sodium, classifying it as a low-sodium food.

Celery Doodles

A delicately browned and less sweet cookie.

3 DOZEN

2 eggs	1/2 teaspoon salt
2 tablespoons skim milk	1/2 teaspoon cinnamon
1 1/2 cups sugar	1/2 teaspoon vanilla flavoring
3/4 cup oil	1 teaspoon lemon extract*
3 cups all-purpose flour	2 cups finely chopped celery
1/2 teaspoon soda	3/4 cup wheat germ
1 teaspoon baking powder	Cinnamon

Preheat oven to 350°. Blend together eggs, milk, sugar, and oil. Sift dry ingredients together and stir into egg mixture. Add vanilla flavoring and lemon extract. Fold in celery and wheat germ; mix thoroughly. If dough is stiff, add more milk, one tablespoon at a time. Drop batter onto ungreased baking sheet, making small cookies about the size of a silver dollar. Sprinkle lightly with cinnamon. Bake for 13 to 15 minutes, or until a delicate brown.

*For a different flavor, use 1 1/2 teaspoons anise extract.

Nutrition Facts (per serving)

Serving size 1 cookie (33g); Servings per recipe 36; Calories 115; Calories from Fat 45; Total Fat 5g (8% DV); Saturated Fat 1g (5% DV); Cholesterol 15mg (5% DV); Vitamin A 0; Vitamin C 1% DV; Sodium 60mg (3% DV); Total Carbohydrate 17g (6% DV); Dietary Fiber 1g (4% DV); Protein 1g; Calcium 1% DV; Iron 3% DV

Polly's Applesauce Cake

A new ingredient enhances a dear friend's spice cake.

16 SERVINGS

Nonstick vegetable cooking spray	*1 teaspoon baking powder*
2 cups sugar	*1/2 teaspoon nutmeg*
1/2 cup shortening	*2 teaspoons cinnamon*
1 1/2 cups applesauce	*1 teaspoon cloves*
1 1/2 cups chopped celery	*1/2 cup chopped walnuts*
1 cup cold water	*1 cup raisins, plumped* (optional)*
3 1/2 cups all-purpose flour	*Quick Maple Icing (recipe follows)*
2 teaspoons baking soda	

Preheat oven to 350°. Spray a 9-inch x 13-inch pan and set aside. Cream together sugar and shortening. Add applesauce, celery, and water. Sift dry ingredients together and fold into batter. Fold in nuts and raisins (optional). Pour batter into prepared pan and bake for 30 to 45 minutes or until toothpick inserted in center comes out clean. Cool on rack. Frost with Quick Maple Icing. Cut into 16 pieces (4 by 4).

*TIP: To plump raisins, soak them in 1 cup water for 10 minutes. Drain thoroughly, saving water. Use that water for the 1 cup of water needed in the recipe.

Quick Maple Icing

3 tablespoons margarine	*1 teaspoon maple flavoring*
2 cups sifted powdered sugar	*3 tablespoons skim milk*

In a medium bowl, mix margarine and powdered sugar. Add flavoring and milk and beat until frosting is uniformly smooth and creamy for easy spreading. If more milk is needed add one or two teaspoons at a time.

Nutrition Facts (per serving)

Serving size 1 piece (140g); Servings per recipe 16; Calories 385; Calories from Fat 99; Total Fat 11g (17% DV); Saturated Fat 2g (10% DV); Cholesterol 0; Vitamin A 2% DV; Vitamin C 3% DV; Sodium 160mg (7% DV); Total Carbohydrate 69g (23% DV); Dietary Fiber 2g (8% DV); Protein 4g; Calcium 3% DV; Iron 9% DV

Corn

HISTORY

European explorers of the 15th and 16th centuries returned from the New World of the Americas with golden kernels far more valuable than the gold nuggets they thought they were seeking. Today corn is one of the world's four principal crops—along with wheat, rice, and potatoes.

It's hard to imagine that corn was unknown to Europeans, Asians, and Africans until only 500 years ago. In the Americas, corn had been cultivated for 8,000 years before the arrival of Christopher Columbus. This grain, that we eat like a vegetable when it is still "green," originated on the eastern slopes of the Andes mountains and spread across South, Central, and North America, including the islands of the Caribbean. Corn sustained great civilizations and nomadic native tribes.

Corn was a vital part of life and legend in the Western Hemisphere. According to a Mayan myth, when the earth goddess visited the sky god one day, she secretly stole a single kernel of corn. To hide her theft, she buried the kernel in the earth. The gods searched high and low for their missing corn kernel but could not find the stolen treasure. When Quetzalcoatl learned that a red ant had seen the earth goddess hide the golden kernel, he turned himself into a black ant and became friends with the red ant. Soon he learned the secret location of the corn. He retrieved it and gave it to humans and taught them how to plant and grow it.

A Cherokee legend tells of a time long ago when humans had only meat and wild fruits to eat. A season of hunger came and there were no animals to be found in the forest. Birds had eaten all the wild fruits before they could even ripen. As the native Americans sat, weak with hunger, around their campfire, a cloud descended from the sky and out stepped a golden-haired maiden dressed in a flowing green robe. One of the young men of the tribe stepped forward to greet her but she vanished the moment his hand touched her arm. Where she had stood was a tall cornstalk, the first one in the world. Her golden hair was the silk, her flowing green robe the leaves, and her toes the roots.

A third story describing the origin of corn comes from the Onondaga tribe. Hiawatha wanted to serve his people. To prepare himself he went into the forest and fasted and prayed to the Great Spirit for four long days. At sunset on the final day, a handsome, flaxen-haired young man in brilliant green clothing and a tasseled headdress suddenly appeared. The stranger invited Hiawatha to wrestle. Weak with hunger though he was, Hiawatha summoned all his strength. They wrestled until darkness fell, with no winner. The stranger disappeared, saying "I will come again tomorrow." The next day Hiawatha and the young man wrestled from sunrise to sunset, again with no winner. On the third day when the stranger appeared again, Hiawatha was prepared to continue the contest, but the golden-haired, green-clad young man announced, "You have proven your courage and strength. Today we will wrestle one final time, but you will win. After I have been defeated, bury me in soft earth and keep my grave free of weeds. Watch and wait, and your people will receive the great gift you seek for them." Hiawatha did as the stranger asked, carefully tending the grave. Rain fell and a tiny green shoot appeared above the grave. Each day the spear grew until it stood tall and straight, dressed in green, with golden hair and a tasseled headdress. In the autumn, Hiawatha's grateful people gathered the wonderful gift, a food treasure from the Great Spirit.

As these stories show, corn was central to nearly all native American tribal cultures. They had a variety of religious festivals of thanksgiving for the corn harvest. Sacrifices of corn bread were offered by Virgins of the Sun in Mexico.

Corn also plays a starring role in one of the unique holidays of the United States. The early American colonists probably would not have survived without corn. That first winter the Plymouth colony was sustained by gifts of corn from the native Americans. The next spring, following instructions from the native

Americans, the surviving colonists planted this unfamiliar food. Their gratitude for the abundant harvest the following autumn led to the feast that we now consider the first United States Thanksgiving celebration. A brass plaque on a Cape Cod monument carries these words from Governor Bradford of the Massachusetts colony: "And sure it was God's good providence that we found this corne for we know not how else we should have done."

SEASON

Fresh sweet corn can often be found in supermarkets all year round, but the peak supply and best prices run early May until mid-September. Frozen or canned kernel corn is a convenient and inexpensive way to have this grain-vegetable all year long.

QUALITY AND STORAGE

When shopping for fresh corn, look for ears that have been kept refrigerated. The sugar in corn is converted to starch as the corn matures. Warm temperatures speed up this process and cool temperatures delay it. Look for fresh, succulent husks with good green color. Check that silk ends are free from decay or worm injury. Carefully pull back a strip of husk to inspect the kernels. Kernels should be tightly packed and plump but not over-mature. Pop a kernel with your fingernail. Milky juice should run out. If the skin of the kernel is tough or the milk gluey, the corn is overripe.

Fresh sweet corn does not store well. The longer it is held after harvest, the more the natural sugars will turn to starch, decreasing flavor and tenderness. If you cannot use them right away, refrigerate the ears. Keeping them in their husks helps to retain moisture. You may also put them into a plastic bag that is loosely closed.

If you are buying frozen or canned corn, check the Nutrition Facts food label. Choose a brand that is low in sodium.

NUTRITIONAL QUALITY

Corn is rich in protein and carbohydrate and has sustained great civilizations as a major foodstuff. Corn is weak in one of the essential amino acids, tryptophan, and in one of the water-soluble vitamins, niacin. However, these are not nutrients of concern in the mixed diets of today's North Americans, and they are readily available in the other foods we eat.

Corn makes minor but worthwhile contributions of a variety of essential minerals and vitamins. One of the great nutritional values of corn is the dietary fiber content. One cup of corn provides 24% of the Daily Value for fiber, considerably more than almost any other vegetable. Fiber is beneficial for gastrointestinal function, for reducing risk of cancer and heart disease, and for assisting in management of body weight.

Apple Corn Fritters

Biscuit mix makes this tempting dessert fast and easy.

20 SERVINGS

Oil for deep fat frying

2 eggs, beaten

1/2 cup sugar

1 teaspoon cinnamon

1/2 teaspoon nutmeg

2 cups applesauce

1 cup whole kernel corn, fresh, frozen, or canned

1/4 cup wheat germ

1/2 teaspoon baking powder

2 cups biscuit mix

Maple-flavored syrup or powdered sugar (optional)

In a large saucepan, preheat 2 to 3 inches of oil to about 375°. Mix eggs, sugar, spices, applesauce, and corn. Stir in wheat germ, followed by baking powder and biscuit mix. Mix just until blended. Do not overmix. For each fritter, drop 1/4 cup batter into the hot oil. Cook about 4 minutes, then turn and continue cooking about 4 more minutes. Serve warm. Drizzle with warm maple-flavored syrup, or sprinkle with powdered sugar, if desired.

Nutrition Facts (per serving)

Serving size 1 fritter (63g); Servings per recipe 20; Calories 140; Calories from Fat 54; Total Fat 6g (9% DV); Saturated Fat 1g (5% DV); Cholesterol 28mg (9% DV); Vitamin A 3% DV; Vitamin C 4% DV; Sodium 228mg (9% DV); Total Carbohydrate 20g (7% DV); Dietary Fiber 2g (8% DV); Protein 2g; Calcium 1% DV; Iron 5% DV

Cucumbers

HISTORY

This cool, refreshing member of the melon family can trace its genealogy back to the Bible. During the exodus of the Israelites from slavery in Egypt, they wandered in the wilderness for 40 years. Well-fed on manna but bored with the unvarying diet, they looked back to Egypt with longing and complained about missing their cucumbers. Delicious and cooling to the desert-parched tongue, cucumbers were raised by the Israelites as soon as they settled in their new land. The prophet Isaiah implied the prized status of cucumbers when he compared the daughter of Zion to "a cottage in a vineyard or a lodge in a garden of cucumbers." The Jews built little huts or lodges in their cucumber fields and stayed there all night each night until harvest in order to drive away night animals or thieving neighbors who would try to raid the precious crop.

The Roman emperor Tiberius ate cucumbers every day of the year. These curved, horn-shaped melons were called cucumis by the Romans. The Latin word meant "curved."

Folklore of the old Britons said that cows were extremely fond of cucumbers, and so the slender, green melon was often called a cowcumber. One superstition said that cucumbers must be gathered only during the full of the moon. Another superstition held that to dream of cucumbers meant you would soon fall in love. Cucumbers grew in the garden of Charlemagne. The cooling properties were recognized by the English writer who said, "rawe or greene cucumbers are fittest for the hotter time of the yeare and for hot stomackes, and not to be used in colder weather or cold stomackes." An old saying that is still used describes a person with striking self-control as being "cool as a cucumber."

Cucumbers were once believed to be poisonous. When that mistaken belief was laid to rest, cucumbers gained value as cures for a host of ailments. Sick, feverish children were placed on a bed of sliced cucumbers. A cure for a cough was cucumber seeds crushed into wine. No doubt it was the alcohol, not the cucumber, that relaxed the muscles and eased the cough!

This vegetable has a special meaning for one noble Japanese family. Long, long ago, a prince, strolling through his garden, stooped to pick a cucumber. To his surprise a tiny man was sitting on one of the green leaves. "I am the genie of the cucumber," he said. "Please don't pick the cucumber. I will make a bargain with you." The Japanese prince was so surprised he couldn't speak. "If you and all your family promise never to eat another cucumber throughout your lifetime," continued the genie, "I will protect you and all your descendants forever." The prince readily agreed. In honor of the bargain, to this day, the cucumber appears on the family's coat of arms.

Although this vegetable is one of the few usually eaten raw, it is actually more digestible when lightly cooked as is common in Middle Eastern cuisines. People who cannot tolerate raw cucumbers can usually enjoy them cooked.

SEASON

Cucumbers are grown in southern states and in Mexico year-round but are at their best and least expensive from May through August. Some specialty varieties are available only during a limited season.

QUALITY AND STORAGE

Choose cucumbers that are bright, lustrous green. Don't be misled by the wax that is commonly applied to supermarket cucumbers. Look for cucumbers that are rigid and well-shaped. Avoid overdeveloped cucumbers. The large, thick vegetables will be seedy and have watery, tasteless flesh. Young, immature cucumbers will have a firm, crisp flesh.

Store in the refrigerator in the crisper drawer to retain moisture. Cucumbers will wilt and grow limp if not kept cool. With proper storage, cucumbers will retain their freshness for several days.

NUTRITIONAL QUALITY

Water, water, water. Cucumbers are 96 percent water and so they are extremely low in calories. One whole cucumber has fewer than 40 calories. There aren't big doses of vitamins and minerals in a cucumber either. But then again, there's no fat at all, no cholesterol, and almost no sodium in a cucumber. Fiber content is modest. It's about as close to a drink of cool, refreshing, life-giving water as a vegetable can get.

Confetti Cookies

The colors creating the flavor also created the name.

34 (2-COOKIE) SERVINGS

3/4 cup margarine, softened	1/2 teaspoon baking soda
3/4 cup sugar	2 teaspoons cinnamon
1 egg	1/4 teaspoon nutmeg
1 teaspoon vanilla flavoring	1 cup grated, unpeeled cucumber
2 cups all-purpose flour	1 cup shredded carrots
2 teaspoons baking powder	3/4 cup raisins

Preheat oven to 375°. Beat together margarine and sugar. Add egg and beat until well blended. Stir in vanilla. Sift the flour, baking powder, baking soda, cinnamon, and nutmeg into batter; mix thoroughly. Stir in cucumber, carrots, and raisins. Drop by teaspoonfuls onto ungreased baking sheet. Bake for 15 to 17 minutes, or until delicate golden brown.

Nutrition Facts (per serving)

Serving size 2 cookies (28g); Servings per recipe 34; Calories 94; Calories from Fat 36; Total Fat 4g (6% DV); Saturated Fat 1g (5% DV); Cholesterol 8mg (3% DV); Vitamin A 22% DV; Vitamin C 1% DV; Sodium 82mg (3% DV); Total Carbohydrate 13g (4% DV); Dietary Fiber 1g (4% DV); Protein 1g; Calcium 1% DV; Iron 3% DV

Zip Chip Bars

In a zip you can have this chip bar ready to enjoy!

12 SERVINGS

Nonstick vegetable cooking spray

1/3 cup margarine

1/2 cup brown sugar

1 egg

1 teaspoon black walnut flavoring*

1 cup all-purpose flour

1/2 cup wheat germ

3/4 teaspoon baking powder

1/4 teaspoon salt

1 cup grated, unpeeled cucumber

1/2 cup mini-morsel chocolate
  chips**

Powdered sugar

Spray an 8-inch round, 2-inch deep microwave dish with cooking spray. Beat together margarine and brown sugar; add egg and beat until smooth. Stir in black walnut flavoring. Mix together flour, wheat germ, baking powder, and salt; stir into batter. Stir in cucumber and chips. Pour into microwave dish. Bake at 30 percent power for 6 minutes, then on full power 3 1/2 to 6 minutes. Rotate dish once or twice if your oven doesn't have a turntable. Bars are done when they no longer look moist on top and pull away from dish edges. Dust with powdered sugar. Cut as you would a pie for 6, and then divide that by cutting into 6 more, giving 12 delicious servings.

TIP: Bars can be baked in a conventional oven for 25 minutes at 350°.

*TIP: Be sure to use the black walnut flavoring. It's the key to the pleasing blend of flavors.

**TIP: Look for color-coated mini-chips in the supermarket. Kids of all ages will enjoy the color splash.

Nutrition Facts (per serving)

Serving size 1 bar (53g); Servings per recipe 12; Calories 185; Calories from Fat 72; Total Fat 8g (12% DV); Saturated Fat 3g (15% DV); Cholesterol 23mg (8% DV); Vitamin A 10% DV; Vitamin C 6% DV; Sodium 193mg (8% DV); Total Carbohydrate 26g (9% DV); Dietary Fiber 2g (8% DV); Protein 3g; Calcium 2% DV; Iron 11% DV

Chocolate Lover's Cake

Lower in fat and higher in fiber than ordinary
chocolate cakes, a treasure for all chocolate lovers.

24 SERVINGS

2 1/2 cups all-purpose flour

3/4 cup cocoa

2 1/2 teaspoons baking powder

1 1/2 teaspoons baking soda

1 teaspoon salt

1 teaspoon cinnamon

3/4 cup soft margarine

2 cups sugar

3 eggs

2 teaspoons vanilla flavoring

2 teaspoons grated orange peel

2 cups coarsely shredded, unpeeled
   cucumber

1/2 cup skim milk

1 cup chopped nuts

Vanilla Glaze (recipe follows)

Preheat oven to 350°. Combine flour, cocoa, baking powder, soda, salt, and cinnamon; set aside. With mixer beat margarine and sugar until smoothly blended. Add eggs one at a time, beating after each addition. Fold in vanilla flavoring, orange peel, and cucumber. Alternately stir in dry ingredients and milk. Add nuts; pour batter into lightly greased and floured 10-inch tube pan or Bundt pan. Bake one hour or until cake tester comes out clean. Cool in pan 15 minutes; turn out on wire rack to cool thoroughly. Drizzle glaze over cake and slice thinly to serve.

Vanilla Glaze

2 cups powdered sugar

1 teaspoon vanilla extract

3 tablespoons skim milk

Combine all ingredients and beat until smooth. Drizzle over cake.

Nutrition Facts (per serving)

Serving size 1 slice (70g); Servings per recipe 24; Calories 245; Calories from Fat 90; Total Fat 10g (15% DV); Saturated Fat 2g (10% DV); Cholesterol 34mg (11% DV); Vitamin A 6% DV; Vitamin C 1% DV; Sodium 255mg (11% DV); Total Carbohydrate 38g (13% DV); Dietary Fiber 1g (4% DV); Protein 3g; Calcium 3% DV; Iron 7% DV

Garlic

HISTORY

Garlic has been used for thousands of years. It was one of the first vegetables enjoyed by the ancient Chinese, so long ago, in fact, that when the written language developed, a single ideogram was used for the pungent food. For many centuries and in many cultures, garlic was popular among the peasants and disdained by the upper classes.

The class distinction was clear in ancient Egypt. Priests considered it unclean, and one who had eaten garlic was not worthy to enter a temple to worship the earth goddess. On the other hand, the slaves who built the Great Pyramid at Giza lived mainly on garlic and onions and went on strike when deprived of their garlic ration. After their exodus from Egypt, the Israelites wandered in the Sinai desert for 40 years. They longed for the foods they had left behind in Egypt, "the leeks, and the onions, and the garlic."

The Greeks loved garlic. Galen, the great physician, used it as a general panacea—to treat dog, spider, scorpion, and snake bites, and as an antidote to all poisons. Roman laborers ate garlic to make them strong. Roman soldiers ate garlic to boost their courage.

Garlic was important in Anglo-Saxon medicine for a variety of situations. It was eaten to keep the elves away, to help you resist demonic temptations, to cure styes, and to treat swellings. In the Middle Ages, garlic became a well-known defense against werewolves, witches, vampires and the evil eye. Garlic was sometimes carried as a good luck charm.

Not only may garlic keep away vampires, it may be useful in the garden. It is said that the liquid in which garlic has been boiled is a safe and effective insecticide spray.

The city of Chicago is named for the wild garlic that once grew there. Native Americans called the area "Chicagoua" for the pungent plant that was abundant in the woods along the shores of the river and great lake. They gathered the herb for cooking and for treating infections.

Garlic contains the amino acid alliin, which has antiseptic qualities that have been used not only by native Americans but also by other peoples throughout the ages. During World War I garlic was used in field hospitals when no other antiseptic was available. And as recently as 1963 the Russians sent out a call for additional garlic to help control a raging flu epidemic.

Although garlic was a favored flavor among southern peoples, it gained slow acceptance as a food by northern peoples. An English writer said in 1699, "We absolutely forbid it entrance into our salads, by reason of its intolerable rankness." Part of a criminal's punishment in old England was to have to eat raw garlic.

After being loved by people for centuries, garlic suffered a decline in popularity in the early 20th century. While immigrants to America continued to savor their garlic, the old established families looked on it as slightly improper. For a time it was difficult to find garlic in the stores and markets. But beginning in the middle of this century, garlic has made a splendid comeback and is now more popular than ever.

In Gilroy, California, during the last week of July each year, you can attend the Gilroy Garlic Festival, watch as the new Garlic Queen is crowned, enjoy the open air entertainment, and witness the incredible Garlic Cookoff. You will have a chance to sample garlic in everything from salad dressings and roasted chicken to cookies and ice cream.

According to popular belief, eating a raw green bean or some parsley after eating garlic will neutralize its odor. Other tricks that garlic-lovers swear by include rinsing your mouth with lemon juice, eating lime sherbet for dessert, or chewing on a coffee bean.

SEASON

Because garlic keeps well, it is never out of season. The new crop is harvested in June through early September. After harvest, bulbs are cured about 3 weeks before being shipped to market.

QUALITY AND STORAGE

Although over half the garlic grown in the United States is dehydrated, the finest flavor comes from the fresh bulbs. You will find garlic sold in bulk, in small packages, or in small mesh bags containing two or three bulbs. Each bulb is composed of 8 to 12 sections called cloves, which are held together by a parchment-like covering.

At the store or market look for firm, plump bulbs, with clean, dry, unbroken skins. Avoid soft, spongy, or shriveled bulbs. Large bulbs have large cloves, but smaller bulbs are just as high in quality and flavor, and may actually be less expensive. At home, garlic stores well in a dry, cool place in an open container. Refrigeration is not recommended because the moisture in a refrigerator makes the cloves spoil too quickly.

Fresh garlic can be frozen for instant convenience. Peel the cloves, then place in a zipper-type plastic bag or an air-tight container and freeze. Unpeeled bulbs of garlic can also be frozen. Just remove cloves as needed.

To peel a clove easily, zap it in the microwave for 20 seconds to loosen the skin. Alternatively, hold the clove upright against a cutting board and hit the clove smartly with the flat side of a heavy knife blade. The sudden pressure loosens the skin. To begin peeling, cut across the root end and peel the skin up toward the other end.

NUTRITIONAL QUALITY

One clove of garlic has only 4 calories. A whole bulb (10 cloves) has small but useful amounts of calcium and potassium, and more vitamin C than an apple.

Garlic is under intense study today in medical laboratories. Folk medicine claims that it can lower blood cholesterol, reduce high blood pressure, prevent cancer, and ease arthritis are being tested. While at the present time, there is no convincing evidence that garlic is a miracle cure for any of these problems, serious research may find some answers soon. The National Cancer Institute has invested $20 million in studies examining the cancer-preventing potential of specific foods like garlic, licorice, and soybeans. John Milner at Pennsylvania State University is studying the prevention of breast cancer through eating garlic. His early research suggests that garlic may block the binding of cancer-causing chemicals to the DNA in cells, the process by which cells are often changed from normal to cancerous. John Pinto at Memorial Sloan Kettering Cancer Center in New York has reported that two sulfur-containing compounds in garlic can fight breast cancer in a test tube.

Honey Garlic Ice Cream

The subtle flavor will mystify your guests.

8 SERVINGS

4 large garlic cloves, peeled

2/3 cup light golden honey

1 quart premium vanilla ice cream, softened

2 to 3 teaspoons finely minced, crystallized ginger*

Put garlic and honey in a heavy saucepan over medium heat. Monitor carefully to avoid honey caramelizing. When it reaches a simmer, remove from heat and cover the pan. Allow garlic to steep overnight.

Remove garlic from honey and discard. Stir honey through softened ice cream, pack into a quart freezer container, and return to freezer. Allow ice cream to remain in freezer at least 24 hours for flavors to blend. Serve garnished with ginger.

*TIP: Use a coffee grinder, sharp chef's knife, or miniature food processor.

Nutrition Facts (per serving)

Serving size 1/2 cup (103g); Servings per recipe 8; Calories 260; Calories from Fat 108; Total Fat 12g (18% DV); Saturated Fat 7g (35% DV); Cholesterol 45mg (15% DV); Vitamin A 9% DV; Vitamin C 1% DV; Sodium 55mg (2% DV); Total Carbohydrate 39g (13% DV); Dietary Fiber 0; Protein 2g; Calcium 8% DV; Iron 1% DV

Greens

HISTORY

Greens is a catchall category of leafy vegetables that are usually eaten cooked rather than raw. Greens traditionally include mustard greens, bok choy, collards, kale, turnip greens, and spinach. A core food in the Southern United States, Africa, and Asia, greens have been less popular in other cooking traditions. With today's emphasis on light, fresh foods, greens are growing in popularity. Trend-setting restaurants are offering cooked greens in place of the too-common peas, beans, and corn.

Greens were probably one of the first vegetables used by humans during their hunter-gatherer stage of development. Even today, wild foods enthusiasts gather and enjoy greens.

Kale grows well in northern climates and was once so valued in Scotland that a meal was not considered complete without kale soup. A lassie picking kale for the supper-pot might dawdle a bit and pull a kale plant up by the roots. She would then strip its leaves one by one, naming a boyfriend with each leaf. Repeating her three or four favorites, with the last leaf she learned which one would be her husband. Luckily the spell could be broken if she were not happy with the one thus selected. She simply didn't eat the soup made with the leaves from that kale stalk.

Another Scottish tradition is described by the national poet Robert Burns in a poem about Halloween. He depicted young people enacting the first ceremo-nial event of the holiday. With eyes shut, they went hand in hand into the fields and pulled the first kale plant they touched. Its shape and size (big or little, crooked or straight) predicted their future husbands or wives. Next they placed the kale stalk over the door frame of the home. The name of the first person who then entered through the door was the name of the person they would marry.

In Irish legend, fairies ride the kale stalks for horses. When a doubting Cork farmer loudly proclaimed that he didn't believe in fairies, they forced him to ride a kale stalk night after night until he retracted.

Folk medicine had many uses for kale. The juice of the crushed leaves, mixed with vinegar, was a cure for deafness or humming or ringing in the ears. Kale, burnt to ashes and mixed with grease, was a liniment for the aches and pains of old age.

Collards is a variety of kale favored in the southern United States. The roots survive all winter, and in early spring they send up new leaves ready for picking.

Although the ancient Persians called it the "prince of vegetables," spinach is not among the most popular vegetables in North America. The butt of continual jokes, spinach is ironically one of the most nutritious of all human foods. Our name for this glossy, rich-green leafy vegetable comes from the Arabic name for it, ispinaj.

A British book in the middle ages, a guide for practicing herbalists, recom-mended spinach for a sick man's diet and as particularly profitable in the diet of the aged. A 17th century physician said that spinach "breeds good blood and makes the whole body lightsome." That makes a lot of scientific sense today, for we now know spinach to be one of the richest sources of vitamins and minerals of all plant foods.

American children have known for decades the power of spinach since it is the magic potion of Popeye the Sailorman. On a more realistic plane, the leafy veg-etable has been particularly appreciated in developed nations since the 1920s when the vitamins were being discovered. Spinach was quickly noted to be a valu-able source of the newly identified nutrients.

SEASON

Winter-weary humans have always looked forward to spring not only for warmer weather and longer days, but also for the first fresh, tender greens. Today, thanks to excellent transportation, most greens are available year-round. Chard is an exception—you will find it in supermarkets only in April through November. Other greens will have seasonal peaks when prices are most favorable for the consumer. For example, collards and kale are in best supply from January through April. Turnip greens are most abundant from October through March.

QUALITY AND STORAGE

Select crisp, dark green leaves. Look for slightly moist leaves, and avoid wilted or dry, browned leaves. Smaller leaves will have a milder flavor than larger leaves. Store fresh unwashed greens in the refrigerator in a plastic bag. They will keep 3 to 6 days.

NUTRITIONAL QUALITY

The darker green, the higher the vitamin content. Greens are excellent sources of vitamin A, vitamin C, folate, and fiber, four nutrients that are often in poor supply in North American diets. Greens also have significant amounts of calcium. New research is showing that the calcium in greens is absorbed nearly as efficiently as the calcium in dairy products. For those who cannot or will not eat dairy products, greens are especially important.

The vitamin C, beta-carotene (vitamin A), and fiber in greens may protect against cancer. Studies show that people who regularly eat carotene-rich vegetables have lower risks for cancer. Whether it is the carotene or other substances in these vegetables that confer protection is unclear.

As an example of how nutritionally rich the greens are, spinach is an excellent source of calcium, iron, vitamin C, vitamin A, and folate. One-half cup of cooked spinach provides 10% of the Daily Value for calcium, 18% of the Daily Value for iron, 15% of the Daily Value for vitamin C, 147% of the Daily Value for vitamin A, and 66% of the Daily Value for folate.

David's Pleasure

*This dessert tastes rather like a lemon sponge pie, the favorite
dessert of a friend, David. Our version has a unique ingredient.*

8 SERVINGS

3 eggs, separated

1 1/4 cups sugar

2 tablespoons margarine

3 tablespoons flour

Grated rind and juice of 2 lemons

1 cup evaporated skim milk

9-inch deep-dish pastry shell,
  homemade, refrigerated, or frozen

1 1/2 teaspoons margarine, divided

16-ounce can turnip greens, *
  drained, rinsed, and drained
  again

3 tablespoons brown sugar, divided

1/3 cup walnuts, chopped

Low-fat whipped topping

Preheat oven to 450°. Beat egg whites until stiff, but not dry, and will hold a peak.
Set aside. Beat sugar and margarine together; add yolks one at a time to sugar
mixture, beating after each addition. Stir in flour, lemon peel, lemon juice, and
evaporated skim milk. Gently fold egg whites into lemon batter. Ladle half of
mixed batter into pie shell.

Using a non-stick skillet, melt 1 teaspoon of the margarine and sauté greens until
quite dry. Add 2 tablespoons of the brown sugar and sauté until partially
caramelized. Place in food processor and chop or puree to cut greens to your pref-
erence. Set aside.

Using the same skillet, sauté nuts in remaining 1/2 teaspoon margarine. Stir in
remaining 1 tablespoon brown sugar and continue stirring until nuts are coated.
Turn out onto paper towel to cool.

Fold nuts and greens together. Drop by tablespoonfuls into lemon batter. Using a
knife or spatula, pull greens lightly through batter.

Top with remaining lemon batter. Bake for 10 minutes; reduce oven temperature
to 325° and continue baking for 20 additional minutes or until filling sets and top
is browned. Allow to cool before serving. Top with a large dollop of low-fat
whipped topping.

*TIP: Fresh spinach greens can also be used. Fresh greens have a 50 percent loss
during cooking, so use twice as much fresh as canned.

Nutrition Facts (per serving)

Serving size 1 wedge (175g); Servings per recipe 8; Calories 390; Calories from Fat 144; Total Fat 16g (25% DV); Saturated Fat 3g (15% DV); Cholesterol 104mg (19% DV); Vitamin A 72% DV; Vitamin C 29% DV; Sodium 245mg (10% DV); Total Carbohydrate 56g (19% DV); Dietary Fiber 2g (8% DV); Protein 9g; Calcium 18% DV; Iron 13% DV

Curious Lemon Cake

*Flavor as fresh as a spring breeze. Everyone will love it! This beautiful
layered cake is truly easy; using a cake mix makes it a snap!*

16 SERVINGS

16 ounces fresh spinach greens *

2 1/2 teaspoons margarine, divided

3 tablespoons brown sugar, divided

Dash of salt

1/3 cup walnuts, chopped

Nonstick vegetable cooking spray

18.25-ounce lemon cake mix

1 1/3 cups water

2 eggs

Tart Lemon Frosting

(recipe follows)

Steam greens for about 5 minutes. Plunge into cold water and drain. Melt 2 teaspoons margarine in non-stick skillet and sauté greens until quite dry. Add 2
tablespoons brown sugar and dash of salt and sauté until partially caramelized.
Remove from skillet and place in food processor; chop to cut greens finely.

In same skillet melt 1/2 teaspoon margarine and sauté nuts. Stir in 1 tablespoon
brown sugar and continue stirring until nuts are coated. Place on paper towel to
cool.

Preheat oven to 350°. Spray two 9-inch round cake pans with cooking spray and
set aside. In a large mixing bowl combine cake mix, water, and eggs. Beat with an
electric mixer until well blended, scraping beaters and sides of bowl often. Beat 3
minutes at high speed. Pour one-third of the batter into each pan, reserving one-
third for final step.

Fold walnuts and greens together. Divide mixture in half and drop by tablespoonfuls into each cake pan. With a knife or spatula pull greens though batter.
Top with remaining cake batter and bake for 30 to 35 minutes, or until toothpick
inserted in center comes out clean. Cool and frost with Tart Lemon Frosting.

*TIP: Canned or frozen greens can also be used. Fresh greens have a 50 percent
loss of volume during cooking so use half as much canned or frozen as fresh.

Tart Lemon Frosting

3 tablespoons margarine

2 cups sifted powdered sugar

1 teaspoon vanilla extract

2 tablespoons lemon juice

1/2 teaspoon lemon extract

Dash salt

Yellow food coloring (optional)

Cream together margarine and powdered sugar until well blended. Add vanilla extract, lemon juice, lemon extract, salt, and food coloring. Beat with electric mixer until smooth and creamy. Put frosting between layers and then frost top and sides of cake.

Nutrition Facts (per serving)

Serving size 1 piece (130g); Servings per recipe 16; Calories 245; Calories from Fat 63; Total Fat 7g (11% DV); Saturated Fat 1g (5% DV); Cholesterol 34mg (11% DV); Vitamin A 40% DV; Vitamin C 14% DV; Sodium 310mg (13% DV); Total Carbohydrate 44g (15% DV); Dietary Fiber 2g (8% DV); Protein 4g; Calcium 9% DV; Iron 9% DV

Jicama

HISTORY

Jicama *(HIC-a-ma)* is an "exotic" vegetable from Mexico that is appearing regularly even in markets in small U.S. midwestern towns. A tuber that can weigh 1 to 6 pounds, jicama looks like a cross between a gigantic turnip and a potato. But this firm, juicy, white-fleshed vegetable tastes like a cross between fresh, sweet pea pods and juicy, crisp water chestnuts.

Jicama is one of the "forgotten roots of the Incas." When the conquistadors came seeking gold and silver, they overlooked some of the great treasures of the Incan civilization. Thinking the Inca people to be primitive, the European conquerors rejected many of their wonderful foods. Only in the past decade have we begun to taste some of the sustaining foods of this once great civilization.

Jicama is much loved in Central America and the Philippines. North American consumers in the know are now seeking out this crisp, refreshing vegetable in the supermarket. They know it's a great low-calorie snack and salad ingredient. Its mild flavor also makes it a terrific ingredient for crunchy desserts.

SEASON

Jicama is available year-round. Look for it in the exotic vegetable section in your supermarket.

QUALITY AND STORAGE

Look for hard, unblemished, well-formed tubers. The skin should be light brown. Avoid roots that are beginning to wrinkle and shrink. They have lost too much moisture in shipping and are poor quality.

This sturdy vegetable stores exceptionally well. Just pop it into the crisper drawer of the refrigerator and use within 1 to 2 weeks.

NUTRITIONAL QUALITY

Like a potato, the jicama is a good source of complex carbohydrates, but it contains more water and less starch, and therefore, fewer calories. Jicama contains a good amount of vitamin C, iron, calcium, and potassium. One half cup of raw, diced jicama has 35 calories, no fat, 25% of the Daily Value for vitamin C, and small amounts of many vitamins and minerals.

Cookie Jar Cookies

A healthful treat to grab from the cookie jar.

4 DOZEN

1/2 cup margarine	*1/2 teaspoon salt*
1 cup light brown sugar	*1 teaspoon cinnamon*
1 egg	*1/2 teaspoon nutmeg*
1 cup wheat germ	*1/4 teaspoon allspice*
1/4 cup skim milk	*2 cups grated jicama*
1 1/2 cups all-purpose flour	*1 cup raisins*
1 teaspoon baking powder	*1/2 cup chopped nuts*

Preheat oven to 375°. Cream margarine and brown sugar; add egg and beat until light. Add wheat germ and milk; mix well. Add dry ingredients and blend together thoroughly. Stir in remaining ingredients. Drop by tablespoonfuls onto greased cookie sheets. Bake about 12 minutes or until golden brown.

Nutrition Facts (per serving)

Serving size 1 cookie (27g); Servings per recipe 48; Calories 85; Calories from Fat 27; Total Fat 3g (5% DV); Saturated Fat 0; Cholesterol 6mg (5% DV); Vitamin A 5% DV; Vitamin C 3% DV; Sodium 85mg (4% DV); Total Carbohydrate 14g (5% DV); Dietary Fiber 2g (8% DV); Protein 2g; Calcium 1% DV; Iron 6% DV

Web of Intrigue Dessert • *page 14*

Maple Sweet Potato Pie • *page* 194

Baked Tropical Dessert • *page* 159

Sliced Green Tomato Pie • *page* 204

Gingerbread in a Pumpkin Shell • *page* 133

Peppered Cocoa Cake • *page* 111
Hot Ice Cream • *page* 109

Orange Spaghetti Cake • *page* 173

Lentils

HISTORY

Cultivated and consumed for centuries, this tiny vegetable is now coming of age in America. The disc-shaped lentil has long been a principal form of nourishment for vegetarian India and for North African peoples. Used since prehistoric times, desiccated lentils have been found in a stone-age site in present-day Hungary and in Egyptian tombs of 2400 B.C. Three of these ancient, preserved lentils are now on display in the Louvre museum in Paris!

Early biblical stories feature lentils. When Esau sold his birthright to younger brother Jacob, he was hungry for a "mess of pottage." The tempting dish has been identified as red lentil porridge. When Daniel and other young Hebrews were captives in the king's court in Babylon, they asked that they be fed not on the rich meats and wines of the king's table, but on pulse, of which the lentil is one example. After a few weeks of the pulse diet, Daniel and the young Hebrew men glowed with good health while the Babylonians seemed pasty and sluggish (Daniel 1:15).

The Romans' name for lentil was lens. Later, a diminutive ending was added to emphasize the smallness of the lentil seed. When a small, round, double-convex piece of glass was invented that made things appear larger, it was named for the round, double-convex vegetable it resembled—the lens.

An ancient Roman myth tells how Venus planned to punish Psyche by setting her the task of separating a mixture of lentils, barley, millet, and vetch into individual piles within just a few hours. A kindly colony of ants came to her rescue, easily and quickly creating four neat piles.

Early Christians had to meet in secret to avoid persecution. One place of secure worship was the underground catacombs. Although they could bring cut flowers in to decorate the altars, they preferred to use living plants in symbolic memory of the resurrection. Only the lentil would sprout and grow a bit in the complete dark of the catacomb. Thus the lentil became an important symbol of Christian hope. Even today, some Christians plant lentils on Ash Wednesday, keep them in a dark closet, and then place them at the foot of the cross in the chapel before Good Friday.

Judges in the late Middle Ages used lentils to assess innocence or guilt of women accused of witchcraft. Dry lentils were floated on water in a bowl. The accused witch swirled the bowl and then was instructed to hold it steady. As the water grew still, the swimming lentils came to rest. If they stopped near the edge of the bowl, she was judged innocent. If the lentils stopped in the center, as if they were trying to avoid her hands, then she was clearly a witch.

SEASON

The U.S. lentil crop comes from the high, dry plateaus of eastern Washington State and northwestern Idaho. Although the new crop of lentils is harvested in the autumn, exceptional storage ability means that the supply is constant all year at a stable price.

QUALITY AND STORAGE

If you are buying packaged lentils, check the bags or boxes to be sure they are undamaged and intact. If the packaging is transparent, look for unbroken discs of consistent color and size. If you are buying in bulk, also look for purity of the lentils. Be aware that small stones, dirt clumps, and plant debris may contaminate the lentils. If the sample is dirty, you will need to wash and sort the lentils before cooking.

NUTRITIONAL QUALITY

Lentils are loaded with nutrients—protein, complex carbohydrates, iron, folate, and fiber. As a bonus, they are also fat free, cholesterol free, and nearly sodium free. For a mere 115 calories, one-half cup of cooked lentils provides 20% of the

Daily Value for protein, 18% of the Daily Value for iron, and 89% of the Daily Value for folate. While most North Americans get plenty of protein in their daily diet (in fact, probably too much), iron and folate are often inadequate. The lentil has a special role as a powerhouse of these two problem nutrients. Iron is needed for healthy red blood and muscles. Iron deficiency makes you weak, tired, and listless. Research has shown that iron-deficient children have reduced learning capacity. Folate is important for building blood as well, but folate has some other important roles, unrecognized until recently. Folate (also known as folacin and folic acid) is vital in the formation of new cells. Inadequate folate leads to poor growth in children and poor maintenance of healthy tissues in children and adults. Accumulating evidence suggests that women who have adequate dietary folate just before and during pregnancy are less likely to have a baby with a neural tube birth defect (spina bifida). An additional health benefit of folate may be a reduction in risk for heart disease. Clearly, choosing folate-rich foods like lentils often is an important contribution to good health, whatever your age.

Lentil Oatmeal Cookies

Great travelers — in a pocket or in a package to one far away.

6 DOZEN

Nonstick vegetable cooking spray

2 cups brown sugar, packed

1 1/2 cups margarine

2 eggs

1 1/2 cups lentil puree (see page XXI)

2 teaspoons vanilla flavoring

3 3/4 cups all-purpose flour

1 teaspoon salt

2 teaspoons baking soda

5 cups quick oats

2 cups chocolate, butterscotch, or peanut butter chips

1 cup chopped walnuts

Preheat oven to 375°. Spray cookie sheets with cooking spray and set aside. Cream together sugar and margarine on medium speed of mixer. Add eggs and mix on low speed until just blended. Add lentil puree and vanilla flavoring and mix until blended. In a separate bowl, mix flour, salt, and baking soda until blended; add to creamed mixture in thirds, mixing on low, just until blended. Mix in oats, chips, and walnuts. Drop dough by teaspoonfuls onto prepared sheet, allowing about 1 inch between each cookie. Bake 12 to 15 minutes, or until puffed lightly and slightly browned. Do not overbake.

Nutrition Facts (per serving)

Serving size 1 cookie (35g); Servings per recipe 72; Calories 140; Calories from Fat 63; Total Fat 7g (11% DV); Saturated Fat 2g (10% DV); Cholesterol 8mg (3% DV); Vitamin A 3% DV; Vitamin C 0; Sodium 100mg (4% DV); Total Carbohydrate 19g (6% DV); Dietary Fiber 1g (4% DV); Protein 2g; Calcium 2% DV; Iron 6% DV

Chocolate Drop Cookies

These cookies freeze and transport very well.
Make them ahead so the flavors can mellow.

9 1/2 DOZEN

Nonstick vegetable cooking spray	*1 teaspoon salt*
4 cups sugar	*1 teaspoon baking powder*
2 1/4 cups margarine	*1 teaspoon baking soda*
4 large eggs	*1 1/4 cups cocoa powder*
3 cups lentil puree (see page XXI)	*2 cups chopped walnuts*
4 teaspoons vanilla flavoring	*Chocolate Buttercream Frosting*
6 1/2 cups all-purpose flour	*(recipe below)*

Preheat oven to 375°. Spray baking sheets with cooking spray and set aside. Cream together sugar and margarine on medium speed of mixer. Add eggs and mix on low speed until just blended. Add lentil puree and vanilla and mix until blended. In a separate bowl mix flour and other dry ingredients until well blended, then add to creamed mixture in thirds, mixing on low speed just until blended. Gently fold in walnuts. Drop by rounded tablespoonfuls on prepared sheets. Bake for 12 to 15 minutes. Do not overbake. Frost with Chocolate Buttercream Frosting, if desired.

Chocolate Buttercream Frosting

2 cups powdered sugar	*1/4 teaspoon salt*
9 tablespoons cocoa powder	*3 tablespoons skim milk*
1/3 cup margarine, softened	*1 teaspoon vanilla extract*

Cream sugar, cocoa, and margarine together until thoroughly blended. Add salt, milk, and vanilla. Beat to a smooth spreading consistency.

Nutrition Facts (per serving)

Serving size 1 cookie (30g); Servings per recipe 112; Calories 125; Calories from Fat 54; Total Fat 6g (9% DV); Saturated Fat 1g (5% DV); Cholesterol 10mg (3% DV); Vitamin A 4% DV; Vitamin C 0; Sodium 85mg (4% DV); Total Carbohydrate 17g (6% DV); Dietary Fiber 1g (4% DV); Protein 2g; Calcium 1% DV; Iron 4% DV

Cocoa Lentil Cake
with Cocoa Mocha Frosting

A chocolate lover's treat.

24 SERVINGS

Nonstick vegetable cooking spray

1 1/2 cups sugar

1 cup oil

2 eggs

1 teaspoon vanilla flavoring

1 3/4 cups lentil puree (see page XXI)

1 cup mashed potatoes, fresh cooked, instant, or leftover

1 cup sifted all-purpose flour

6 tablespoons cocoa powder

1 1/2 teaspoons baking soda

1/2 teaspoon salt

Cocoa Mocha Frosting (recipe follows)

Preheat oven to 350°. Spray a 9-inch x 13-inch pan with cooking spray; set aside. Beat sugar, oil, and eggs for 2 minutes. Add vanilla, lentil puree, and potatoes to the sugar mixture. Add flour, cocoa, baking soda, and salt to the creamed mixture and beat for 2 minutes. Pour into prepared cake pan. Bake for 30 to 35 minutes. Cool, and frost with Cocoa Mocha Frosting.

Cocoa Mocha Frosting

2 cups powdered sugar

1 tablespoon unsweetened cocoa

3 tablespoons soft margarine

1 tablespoon dry instant coffee *

2 tablespoons skim milk

1 teaspoon vanilla extract

Sift powdered sugar and cocoa into a medium-sized bowl. Add softened margarine and beat until smooth and creamy. Add instant coffee and milk; continue beating for about 2 minutes. Add vanilla and beat well.

*TIP: If instant coffee has large granules, crush it in a coffee grinder to a fine powder. (However, some people prefer the "mocha bursts" they get with the larger granules.)

Nutrition Facts (per serving)

Serving size 1 piece (67g); Servings per recipe 24; Calories 225; Calories from Fat 99; Total Fat 11g (17% DV); Saturated Fat 2g (10% DV); Cholesterol 23mg (8% DV); Vitamin A 2% DV; Vitamin C 1% DV; Sodium 165mg (7% DV); Total Carbohydrate 30g (10% DV); Dietary Fiber 2g (8% DV); Protein 3g; Calcium 1% DV; Iron 5% DV

Melons

HISTORY

Melons are schizophrenic. Some are sweet and commonly used for desserts while others are bitter and must be cooked properly to become edible. Cantaloupe, watermelon, honeydew, casaba, and bitter melon—they're all "fruits" with a secret—they're really vegetables.

From the same family as cucumbers and squash, melons originated in Africa. First grown in the middle of the Kalahari Desert, watermelons were a life-giving source of water. Grateful travelers carried the wonderful vegetable from Africa throughout the Mediterranean region, to India and China. Slaves brought melons with them in their forced exodus from Africa to the New World.

The walls of Egyptian tombs were painted with pictures of melons. The ancient Romans carried cantaloupe with them on their conquering way through Europe. Melons were enjoyed by only the elite until the 15th century when they became wildly popular in France. Cantaloupe seeds were carried to America by Columbus.

During the U.S. Civil War the confederate troops boiled watermelon to extract its sugar and molasses. Today Americans eat an average of 13 pounds of watermelon every year. Russians make beer from watermelon juice, while Asians roast melon seeds for snacks.

The world record for watermelon seed spitting is 66 feet 11 inches, set by Jack

Dietz of Chicago, who has won the national watermelon-seed-spitting contest many times. The world record for the largest watermelon is 255 pounds, grown by a gardener in Oklahoma.

SEASON

Cantaloupe is available year-round in North America but you pay a high price during autumn, winter, and spring. Peak supply is June through August. Honeydew is at its best quality and best price from June through October. Watermelon is in season May through October. Melon balls are available year-round, frozen in plastic pouches.

QUALITY AND STORAGE

Choosing the ripest, sweetest melon is an art. Melon lovers favor a variety of methods and argue long and loud over the surest technique. Some scratch the rind with a fingernail. Some shake the melon and listen. Some sniff. Here are suggestions from professional melon growers who want you to get the best they have to offer.

Cantaloupe: Choose melons with golden netting covering a creamy yellow background. A green background indicates an unripe melon. Press on the blossom end (opposite the stem end). It should yield slightly and give you a sweet, musky, flowery smell. Let cantaloupe stand at room temperature 2 to 3 days before using. The flesh will be softer, juicier, and more fragrant.

Honeydew: The perfectly ripened honeydew melon is creamy white, almost pale yellow. Greener honeydews aren't ripe. Sniff, and you should detect a sweet aroma. The rind should have a very slight, oily film.

Watermelon: Look for a watermelon that is symmetrical in shape, without dents, bruises, or cuts. Size is no indication of sweetness, although the melon should feel heavy for its size. The rind should have a healthy sheen and the underside should be yellow. If you want to use the thump method, listen for a dull hollow sound. If the stem is attached it should look dry and brown, indicating the melon had matured. If the stem looks green, the melon was picked too soon.

NUTRITIONAL QUALITY

Melons are real nutritional stars. Like other vegetables, the melons are low in calories, essentially fat free, low in sodium, high in fiber, and rich in vitamins and minerals.

The cantaloupe's orange flesh signals the presence of beta-carotene, the plant form of vitamin A. One cup of cantaloupe cubes has less than 60 calories, 113% of the Daily Value for vitamin C, 103% of the Daily Value for vitamin A, 14% of the Daily Value for folate, and 5% of the Daily Value for dietary fiber. All this outstanding nutrition and good taste, too!

Honeydew has the same low calories as cantaloupe but is lower in vitamin content. One cup of honeydew melon cubes provides 70% of the Daily Value for vitamin C, negligible beta-carotene, folate and dietary fiber, but nearly 30% of the recommended daily potassium.

Watermelon's rosy color suggests the presence of some carotenoids, or the plant's version of vitamin A. Full of pure, refreshing water, the watermelon is the lowest in calories of all melons. One cup of watermelon cubes has only 50 calories. That cup of ruby cubes also provides 25% of the Daily Value for vitamin C, 12% of the Daily Value for vitamin A, 2% of the Daily Value for folate, 2% of the Daily Value for iron, and 3% of the Daily Value for dietary fiber. These nutrient values may look small, but then you only eat 50 calories in order to get them!

Cantaloupe Sorbet

Colorful and refreshing!

8 SERVINGS

1 medium ripe cantaloupe
2 tablespoons lemon juice

1 cup Simple Syrup, cold (recipe
follows)

Halve cantaloupe and remove seeds. Scoop out fruit (about 4 cups). Process in food processor, scraping down sides, until pureed. Combine puree, lemon juice, and Simple Syrup. Place in an ice cream freezer and freeze according to manufacturer's directions. Or pour into a shallow pan or freezer tray and allow to freeze, stirring often to avoid ice crystals.

Simple Syrup

1 cup sugar   *1/2 cup water*

Bring sugar and water to a boil over medium heat, without stirring. Reduce to medium low heat, cover, and simmer 5 minutes without stirring. Remove from heat and allow to cool. Cover and refrigerate. Makes 1 cup. (Syrup can be prepared up to 1 week before using.)

Nutrition Facts (per serving)

Serving size 1/2 cup (180g); Servings per recipe 8; Calories 215; Calories from Fat 0; Total Fat 0; Saturated Fat 0; Cholesterol 0; Vitamin A 43% DV; Vitamin C 50% DV; Sodium 7mg (1% DV); Total Carbohydrate 56g (19% DV); Dietary Fiber 1g (4% DV); Protein 1g; Calcium 1% DV; Iron 1% DV

Seafoam Pie

As refreshing as a summer breeze. Wonderful flavor!

8 SERVINGS

1 tablespoon unflavored gelatin	3 cups low-fat whipped topping,
1/2 cup sugar	thawed
1/4 teaspoon salt	1 1/2 cups cantaloupe cubes,
3 slightly beaten eggs	about 1/2"
1/2 cup lime juice	Baked 9-inch deep-dish pastry shell,
1/4 cup water	refrigerated, homemade or frozen
1 teaspoon grated lime peel	Low-fat whipped topping, for garnish
Few drops green food coloring	1/3 cup toasted sliced almonds

Combine gelatin, sugar, and salt in a saucepan. Stir together eggs, lime juice, and water, and add to gelatin mixture. Cook and stir over medium heat just until mixture comes to a boil. Remove from heat; add lime peel and food coloring. Chill, stirring occasionally, until mixture mounds. Fold gelatin mixture into whipped topping. Carefully fold in melon cubes. Pile into cooled pastry shell. Chill until firm. Top with a ring of low-fat whipped topping and garnish with almonds.

Nutrition Facts (per serving)

Serving size 1 wedge (125g); Servings per recipe 8; Calories 295; Calories from Fat 153; Total Fat 17g (26% DV); Saturated Fat 6g (30% DV); Cholesterol 100mg (34% DV); Vitamin A 26% DV; Vitamin C 31% DV; Sodium 240mg (10% DV); Total Carbohydrate 32g (11% DV); Dietary Fiber 2g (8% DV); Protein 6g; Calcium 4% DV; Iron 7% DV

Melon Berry Glacé Pie

Sparkles with jewel-bright color.

8 SERVINGS

1/2 cup light cream cheese (tub)	1/8 teaspoon salt
1 tablespoon skim milk	1 teaspoon butter flavoring
9-inch baked pie shell	1 teaspoon finely grated lemon peel
1 cup strawberries	Red food color (optional)
1/2 cup water	3 cups diced cantaloupe, drained
1/2 cup sugar	Low-fat topping and 4 strawberries
2 tablespoons cornstarch	for garnish

Beat cream cheese and milk until smooth. Spread over bottom of cooled, baked pie shell. Refrigerate.

Crush strawberries slightly and combine with water; simmer 4 to 5 minutes, then press through sieve. Discard seeds. Blend sugar, cornstarch, and salt; stir into strawberries in a small saucepan. Stirring constantly, bring to a boil. Continue cooking and stirring over low heat 2 minutes until mixture is thickened and translucent. Remove from heat and stir in butter flavoring and lemon peel. Add food coloring if desired. Cool until lukewarm.

Place cantaloupe in pie shell on top of cheese. Spoon strawberry mixture over fruit. Chill for 2 hours before serving. Garnish with a dollop of low-fat whipped topping and a fresh strawberry half.

Nutrition Facts (per serving)

Serving size 1 wedge (105g); Servings per recipe 8; Calories 165; Calories from Fat 90; Total Fat 10g (15% DV); Saturated Fat 3g (15% DV); Cholesterol 6mg (2% DV); Vitamin A 23% DV; Vitamin C 41% DV; Sodium 235mg (10% DV); Total Carbohydrate 18g (6% DV); Dietary Fiber 2g (8% DV); Protein 3g; Calcium 3% DV; Iron 4% DV

Melon Sorbet

A delicate palate-pleaser, without question.

8 SERVINGS

6 cups diced, seeded watermelon or
1/2 large ripe honeydew melon

2 tablespoons lemon juice
1 cup Simple Syrup, cold (page 84)

Remove seeds from melon half. Scoop out fruit. Puree in food processor. Combine puree, lemon juice, and Simple Syrup. Place in an ice cream freezer and freeze according to manufacturer's directions. Or pour into a shallow pan or freezer tray and allow to freeze, stirring often to avoid ice crystals.

Nutrition Facts (per serving)

Serving size 1/2 cup (195g); Servings per recipe 8; Calories 220; Calories from Fat 0; Total Fat 0; Saturated Fat 0; Cholesterol 0; Vitamin A 1% DV; Vitamin C 36% DV; Sodium 9mg (1% DV); Total Carbohydrate 58g (19% DV); Dietary Fiber 0; Protein 1g; Calcium 1% DV; Iron 0

Watermelon Cooler

A light, refreshing summer dessert.

4 SERVINGS

2 cups watermelon balls	*1 pint lemon sherbet*
1 cup blueberries	*1 quart diet gingerale, chilled*

Divide watermelon balls and blueberries among 4 tall glasses. Add 1/2 cup sherbet to each glass. Fill glasses with gingerale.

Nutrition Facts (per serving)

Serving size 1 cup (450g); Servings per recipe 4; Calories 180; Calories from Fat 27; Total Fat 3g (5% DV); Saturated Fat 1g (5% DV); Cholesterol 7mg (2% DV); Vitamin A 9% DV; Vitamin C 24% DV; Sodium 70mg (3% DV); Total Carbohydrate 40g (13% DV); Dietary Fiber 1g (4% DV); Protein 2g; Calcium 7% DV; Iron 3% DV

Watermelon Slyce

*A sly, easy-to-make dessert that will make friends
and family smyle. The ingredients are assembled to make a
dessert that looks like a slice of fresh watermelon!*

16 SERVINGS

Watermelon Sorbet (recipe follows)   *1 pint low-fat vanilla ice cream*
1 quart lime sherbet   *Chocolate chips*

First, make Watermelon Sorbet and freeze.

Press spoonfuls of lime sherbet along inside wall of a 9-inch springform pan, spreading evenly to form about a 2-inch thick layer. (Bottom of pan will remain empty.) Cover pan with plastic wrap and freeze until firm, about 1 hour.

Spoon vanilla ice cream in an even layer over sherbet. Recover pan with plastic wrap and freeze until firm, about 30 minutes.

Spoon freshly-frozen Watermelon Sorbet into center of springform pan, packing sorbet to remove air holes. Smooth top of sorbet level with sherbet and ice cream border. Decorate with chocolate chip "seeds." Recover and freeze until solid, several hours or overnight. To serve, carefully remove sides of springform pan. Slice into wedges and serve immediately.

Watermelon Sorbet

6 cups diced, seeded watermelon   *2 1/2 cups sugar*
1/3 cup lemon juice

In blender or food processor, puree watermelon until liquefied. In large bowl stir together watermelon juice, lemon juice, and sugar until sugar is dissolved. Pour mixture into ice cream maker. Freeze according to manufacturer's instructions. Or pour into shallow tray and freeze, stirring often to prevent formation of large ice crystals.

Nutrition Facts (per serving)

Serving size 1 wedge (185g); Servings per recipe 16; Calories 250; Calories from Fat 27; Total Fat 3g (5% DV); Saturated Fat 2g (10% DV); Cholesterol 6mg (2% DV); Vitamin A 7% DV; Vitamin C 18% DV; Sodium 35mg (2% DV); Total Carbohydrate 57g (19% DV); Dietary Fiber 1g (4% DV); Protein 2g; Calcium 6% DV; Iron 2% DV

Onions

HISTORY

The onion is known as far back as history reaches and is perhaps the most widely grown vegetable in the world. It was first cultivated in Asia and from thence spread to India and Egypt. The onion was considered sacred by the ancient Egyptians and appears frequently in tomb paintings. One mummy was opened to find the corpse clutching an onion in his hand. Common wisdom holds that onions were one of the basic, sustaining foods of the slaves who built the great pyramids.

The onion has been regarded by some cultures as too divine to eat and by others (Indian Brahmins) as too impure to eat.

Onions play a role in a famous drama in ancient Greek myth. King Pirithous concluded, in a decidedly modern fashion, that marrying a daughter of Jupiter might further his career. He chose Proserpine, queen of Hades, and enlisted the help of his friend, Theseus, in the dangerous adventure of kidnapping her from her home in the underworld. Unfortunately for the two raiders, Proserpine's husband, Pluto, knew what was what. He seized them and held them captive. Tender hearted Proserpine sympathized with the two mortals forced to remain among the shades of the dead. Every day she smuggled delicacies to them from Pluto's own table. And what were these choice morsels? Onions.

In the Middle Ages onions were as valuable as gold. One medical writer described them this way. "Boiled, they give a kindly relish, raise appetite, corroborate the stomach and profit the asthmatical." But everyone has his own taste in foods, and an early English writer declared, "Being eaten, yea though it be boyled, the onyon causeth headache, hurteth the eys, and maketh a man dim-sighted, dulleth the sences, and provoketh overmuch sleepe."

The onion's name comes from the Latin word unio, meaning oneness. In contrast to the garlic bulb which is made up of several separate "bulbs," the onion is one, united. And as a united whole with a hidden center, the onion is a frequent symbol for truth-seeking, for eternity and immortality, and for the universe. All of these are like the onion where one can strip away layer after layer and never reach the end. Or one may reach the core and find the truth or find that there is nothing there after all. It's all in the interpretation.

Peer Gynt, the hero of Ibsen's play, said his life was like an onion, it was empty at the core. An old proverb says that onions make a person wink, drink, and stink.

An early medical theory was the Doctrine of Signatures. Plants indicated by their shape their intended purpose. The globular shape of the onion showed that nature obviously intended it for treatment of head ailments. And indeed it was used for centuries as treatment for hearing problems, vision difficulties (ouch!), and baldness. The onion could even awaken a lazy mind to greater achievement.

Much folklore surrounds the onion. To dream of an onion is good luck. If you put an onion under your pillow on the night of the winter solstice, December 21, you will have a vision of your future spouse. Eating a whole raw onion a day will spare you from catching a cold. A thick-skinned crop of onions means a severe winter is ahead.

Can you guess the answer to this Anglo-Saxon riddle?

> I was alive and said nothing, even so I die.
>
> Back I came before I was. Everyone plunders me,
>
> Keeps me confined and shears my head,
>
> Bites my bare body, breaks my sprouts.
>
> No man I bite unless he bites me;
>
> Many there are who do bite me.

Of course, it's an onion.

SEASON

Some onions are always in season, but certain varieties are available only during a limited time each year. Two of the sweetest onions are the Walla Walla onion from Washington State and the Vidalia onion from Georgia. Lovers of these onions know to buy them in quantity when they appear in the market and then to use them quickly, since they don't store well. Vidalia onions are available from late April through mid-July. Walla Walla onions are available only in July and August.

QUALITY AND STORAGE

The best quality fresh onions are firm and well-covered with papery skin. Avoid onions that have nicks, blemishes, damp spots, or signs of mold and decay. There should be no sprouts and the skin should be dry. Onion varieties differ greatly in flavor. Some are sharper and some are sweeter. The Walla Walla and the Vidalia onions are the two sweetest available in the U.S. market. The Vidalia onion, in fact, is so sweet it imparts sweetness to other foods that are cooked with it.

The key to keeping onions fresh is to keep them cool, dry, and separate. Storage in the refrigerator is possible, but takes up precious space. Whole onions can be stored in clean, old pantyhose legs with a knot tied between each onion to keep them separate. Hang the onion-filled pantyhose in a cool, well-ventilated area. Onions can also be stored on racks or screens. Make sure they do not touch, and keep them in a cool place.

NUTRITIONAL QUALITY

One medium onion has only 60 calories along with 20% of the Daily Value for vitamin C, 12% of the Daily Value for dietary fiber, and a generous amount of potassium. An onion also has small amounts of the other vitamins and minerals important for good health. Onions are naturally low in sodium and fat free. Surprisingly, a whole fresh onion has twice the vitamin C of an apple. Cooked, the onion loses some, but not all, of its vitamin C content.

Some studies have suggested that onions lower blood pressure and cholesterol levels, but the research is not conclusive and the quantity of onion needed is probably not realistic. The National Cancer Institute is currently studying the potential for onions to reduce risk of cancer. Preliminary research hinted that vegetables in the onion family lowered the risk of stomach cancer. At this point, nothing is definite, but onions may have health value that was previously unknown.

Spicy Southern Cake

A big cake for a big occasion, and the ingredients are a big surprise.

24 SERVINGS

Nonstick vegetable cooking spray

3 cups sugar

3/4 cup shortening

4 cups grated Vidalia onions
    (about 1 pound)

1 1/2 cups applesauce

1 1/2 cups buttermilk*

5 1/4 cups all-purpose flour

3 teaspoons baking soda

1 1/2 teaspoons baking powder

1/4 teaspoon fresh ground pepper

3/4 teaspoon nutmeg

3 teaspoons cinnamon

1 1/2 teaspoons cloves

1 1/2 cups chopped pecans

1 cup raisins, plumped**

Nutty Frosting (recipe below)

Preheat oven to 350°. Spray three 9-inch round cake pans and set aside. Cream together sugar and shortening. Fold in onions, and applesauce; add buttermilk. Sift dry ingredients together and fold into batter. Add nuts and raisins. Pour batter into prepared pans and bake for 45 minutes. Cool on rack. Spread layers with Nutty Frosting, and stack.

*TIP: Reconstituted powdered buttermilk can be used.

**TIP: To plump raisins, soak them in 1 cup water for 10 minutes; drain thoroughly before adding to batter.

Nutty Frosting

2 cups powdered sugar, sifted

1 cup creamy peanut butter

3 tablespoons skim milk

1 1/2 teaspoons butter flavoring

Beat all ingredients together until smooth and fluffy.

Nutrition Facts (per serving)

Serving size 1 piece (155g); Servings per recipe 24; Calories 450; Calories from Fat 150; Total Fat 17g (26% DV); Saturated Fat 3g (15% DV); Cholesterol 1mg (0% DV); Vitamin A 0; Vitamin C 3% DV; Sodium 195mg (8% DV); Total Carbohydrate 72g (24% DV); Dietary Fiber 4g (16% DV); Protein 8g; Calcium 5% DV; Iron 11% (DV)

Parsnips

HISTORY

Parsnips, members of the carrot family cultivated since at least Roman times, have been a staple of northern peoples for centuries. The sweet, nourishing roots were the main source for carbohydrates until the early 19th century when a newcomer, the potato, displaced them in popularity. Largely unfamiliar in North America today, parsnips deserve a renewed interest. Looking like big, off-white carrots, parsnips are sweet and mild flavored. They have a nutty taste and a celery-like fragrance.

According to folklore, parsnips were poisonous if eaten before the first frost. This, of course, wasn't true. The vegetable just didn't taste as sweet until it was touched with frost.

SEASON

Parsnips are a winter vegetable. Requiring a long growing season, they are harvested after a hard frost in the fall. Freezing temperatures begin converting the parsnip's starches to sugars and producing the favored sweet taste. Some growers leave parsnips in the ground all winter, harvesting as needed. They believe that the parsnips harvested in spring, after spending winter in the ground, are the sweetest of all. Parsnips are available all year but the supply and quality are lowest during the summer.

QUALITY AND STORAGE

Choose well-shaped, firm roots that are not too large. Large parsnips may be woody and tough. Color can range from ivory to pale yellow. Avoid roots that are flabby or show signs of rootlet growth. Blemished roots will have a short storage life and may have much waste as you have to cut away the blemished spots.

Store unwashed parsnips in the refrigerator in a plastic bag. Like other roots, parsnips are good keepers and will retain high quality for up to 3 to 4 weeks if stored in the coldest part of the refrigerator.

Like potatoes, the white flesh of parsnips discolors upon exposure to air. To avoid darkening, don't cut parsnips until you are ready to use them.

NUTRITIONAL QUALITY

Parsnips are a good source of dietary fiber (2 grams per half cup cooked). They provide modest amounts of all the minerals. Parsnips provide a nutritional bargain in that their sweet flavor comes in a low-calorie package. All vegetables are low in calories, but not all are as sweet as parsnips. One-half cup of cooked parsnip provides 22% of the Daily Value for folate and 17% of the Daily Value for vitamin C.

Baked Parsnips and Fruit

This easy dish is a colorful blending of compatible flavors.

6 SERVINGS

1 pound parsnips (4 cups)

2 apples, any cooking variety

1 orange

3 tablespoons melted margarine

2 tablespoons brown sugar

3 tablespoons orange juice

Nonstick vegetable cooking spray

Preheat oven to 325°. Peel parsnips and cut into matchstick strips. Core apples; cut into 8 wedges per apple. Slice unpeeled orange into 1/4-inch slices. In a large bowl, combine margarine, brown sugar, and orange juice. Add parsnips, apples, and orange and mix well to coat. Transfer to a lightly-sprayed baking dish (a 9-inch x 13-inch glass dish is best), cover, and bake for 30 minutes, stirring occasionally. Uncover and bake 15 minutes longer to glaze. Baste with juices and serve warm.

Nutrition Facts (per serving)

Serving size 3/4 cup (215g); Servings per recipe 6; Calories 205; Calories from Fat 54; Total Fat 6g (9% DV); Saturated Fat 1g (5% DV); Cholesterol 0; Vitamin A 6% DV; Vitamin C 54% DV; Sodium 80mg (3% DV); Total Carbohydrate 38g (13% DV); Dietary Fiber 3g (12% DV); Protein 2g; Calcium 6% DV; Iron 5% DV

Peas

HISTORY

Peas were standard, staple foods among the peoples of ancient civilizations. Well-preserved dry peas were found in the excavations of the ancient city of Troy and in other Bronze Age archeological sites. Egyptian tombs have yielded peas, stashed there for the use of the deceased person in the afterlife. Fossilized peas have even been found in the remains of prehistoric lake-dweller villages in Switzerland. The pea is perhaps the oldest known vegetable.

Norse mythology tells the story of how peas came to be. Thor, the God of Thunder, became angry with humankind. To punish them he sent dragons flying through the air, dropping small green pellets into wells. As the pellets rotted they fouled the water, and humans were no longer able to use the vital, life-giving water. But as the dragons flew, dropping the punishing pellets, some fell on land and sprouted and produced delicious peas. To appease Thor, the people dedicated the peas to him and agreed to eat them only on his day, Thursday.

Peas were among the first crops to be planted by the American colonists, who had carried the seeds from England. Peas porridge was once a popular English dish, and most children have learned the nursery rhyme, "Pease porridge hot, pease porridge cold, pease porridge in the pot, nine days old." A traditional Palm Sunday dish in Northern England until recent times was peas, soaked overnight, then fried in butter and sprinkled with rum and sugar.

Because peas were such a basic food and have been used for thousands of years, much folklore has grown up around them. Along the Scottish-English border, people believed that a maiden shelling peas who found nine in a pod was certain not to be a spinster. If she placed the pod over the door frame, she would marry the first single man who entered. Whether he was handsome or kind or whether they would live happily ever after was not part of the pea prediction! Another belief was more specific. To dream of a pea was to foretell marriage. If the pea in your dream was green, then the marriage would be full of perfect happiness.

The pea is a star in a popular fairy tale created by the Danish writer Hans Christian Andersen, "The Princess and the Pea." Popular pea sayings include: "Love and pease porridge are two dangerous things; one breaks the heart and the other the belly." "She went into the pea field," means she went to sleep. "To give a pea for a bean" means an action done now with an eye toward the future.

Thanks to the humble pea, one of the most important scientific discoveries of all time was made. Gregor Mendel (1822-1884) was an Austrian monk who loved gardening. He noticed that some peas, when dried, were wrinkled and some were smooth. He had the interesting idea of keeping track of which kind of peas came from which planted seeds. He also deliberately cross-pollinated pea plants to see what would happen. From his observations, the science of genetics, so important to us today, was born.

Dried peas were inexpensive and could be stored for use during times of famine, want, and winter weather. It is only comparatively recently that peas have been eaten fresh. In the 17th century court of Louis XIV, sweet green peas first gained popularity, but they commanded astronomical prices, so for a long time they remained a delicacy only for the wealthy.

SEASON

Dried peas have no season. They are always available. Fresh green peas, on the other hand, have a very short peak season—April through July. Fresh peas from California and Florida may be found in supermarkets from September to December.

QUALITY AND STORAGE

Since all our recipes use dried, not fresh, peas, the following tips refer to the dried versions. Dried peas come in several varieties: split green peas, split yellow peas, round green peas, and round yellow peas. So-called chick-peas and black-eyed peas are actually beans.

Dried peas may be packaged in clear or opaque plastic bags, boxes, or paper bags. They may also be available in bulk. Check that boxes and bags are undamaged and intact. If you can see the peas, check to be sure they are unbroken and uncracked. Insect damage would appear as pin holes. Inspect dry peas, and remove any broken peas or foreign materials. Rinse peas in cold water before use.

Dried peas store so well it's almost unnecessary to give them any thought. Stored in a sealed container (to keep out insects and rodents) at cool room temperature, dried peas will easily keep for a year. Even longer storage times are reasonable, but the older the peas get, the longer they will take to cook. Also, if they have been stored under hot, humid conditions, they will take longer to cook.

NUTRITIONAL QUALITY

Dried peas are a wonderful source of protein, iron, and fat-free energy. One-half cup of cooked split green peas provides 15% of the Daily Value for protein and 6% of the Daily Value for iron. Dried peas are the least expensive source of protein in North America. It costs nine times as much to get your recommended daily allowance of protein from steak and five times as much from cheese as from dried peas.

Fiber and folate are also abundant in dried peas. One-half cup of cooked split green peas has over 3 grams of dietary fiber or 12% of the Daily Value for fiber. Hardly another natural food can match this value. Folate is a rather hard-to-get nutrient, but recent research is showing how vital it is, so vital that the FDA has issued a plan to fortify foods with it. Look no further. That same 1/2 cup of cooked split peas has a whopping 32% of the Daily Value for folate. What a champion!

Sweet Pea Bars

Olive Oyl could satisfy anyone's sweet tooth with this treat.

24 SERVINGS

2/3 cup dry split peas	1 teaspoon baking soda
2 cups water	1 teaspoon baking powder
1 cup skim milk	1/2 teaspoon cloves
1/4 cup oil	1/2 teaspoon cinnamon
1 cup sugar	1/4 teaspoon salt
2 eggs	1 cup raisins *
2 1/2 cups all-purpose flour, divided	1/4 cup chopped nuts (optional)

Combine split peas and water. Cook about one hour over very low heat to make a thick soup. (Add a little more water if it gets too thick to stir.) Combine thick soup and milk; set aside.

Preheat oven to 350°. In a large mixing bowl combine oil, sugar, and eggs; beat well. Sift 2 cups flour with baking soda, baking powder, spices, and salt. To egg mixture, add sifted ingredients alternately with pea "soup," mixing thoroughly after each addition. Dredge raisins and nuts in remaining 1/2 cup flour and stir into batter. Spread in lightly oiled 9-inch x 13-inch pan; bake for 45 minutes or until evenly browned. Cut into 24 bars (4 by 6).

*TIP: Diced prunes or another dried fruit could be used for variety.

Nutrition Facts (per serving)

Serving size 1 bar (55g); Servings per recipe 24; Calories 150; Calories from Fat 36; Total Fat 4g (6% DV); Saturated Fat 0; Cholesterol 23mg (8% DV); Vitamin A 1% DV; Vitamin C 1% DV; Sodium 85mg (3% DV); Total Carbohydrate 26g (9% DV); Dietary Fiber 1g (4% DV); Protein 3g; Calcium 3% DV; Iron 6% DV

Mint Julep Pie

Like a cool mint julep on a summer's day.

8 SERVINGS

Oatmeal Crust (recipe follows)

1/4 cup sugar

1 1/2 cups split pea puree (see page XXI)

1 teaspoon mint extract

1 teaspoon vanilla extract

1/4 teaspoon salt

3 cups low-fat vanilla ice cream, softened

2 to 3 drops blue food coloring

1/3 cup pecan halves

Combine sugar, puree, flavorings, and salt. Stir softened ice cream. Fold into pureed mixture. Add blue food coloring one drop at a time (if the mixture seems yellowish). Use one or two drops of green if needed to get the mint green shade you desire. Set filling in freezer 12 to 15 minutes. Remove from freezer (outer edge will be firm); stir mixture and return to freezer for about the same length of time. When mixture is fairly thick, pour into cooled Oatmeal Crust. By using a gradual freezing process the pie will have a smoother texture and be less likely to contain ice crystals. Garnish with pecan halves. Cover with plastic wrap and freeze until solid. Allow to stand 10 minutes at room temperature before serving.

Oatmeal Crust

Nonstick vegetable cooking spray

1/4 cup margarine

1 cup quick cooking oats

1/4 cup sugar

1/4 teaspoon cinnamon

Preheat oven to 350°. Spray a 9-inch deep-dish pie pan with cooking spray. Put margarine in pan and melt in oven. Remove from oven when melted and stir in dry ingredients. Bake for 15 minutes. Remove from oven, and with a fork; immediately press mixture to sides and bottom of pan to form a crust. Cool before -filling.

Nutrition Facts (per serving)

Serving size 1/2 cup (115g); Servings per recipe 8; Calories 255; Calories from Fat 108; Total Fat 12g (18% DV); Saturated Fat 3g (15% DV); Cholesterol 7mg (2% DV); Vitamin A 9% DV; Vitamin C 1% DV; Sodium 180mg (8% DV); Total Carbohydrate 35g (12% DV); Dietary Fiber 3g (12% DV); Protein 7g; Calcium 8% DV; Iron 7% DV

Peppers

HISTORY

Peppers are a gift from the New World. Before 1492 no Old World language—not English, French, German, Spanish, or even Latin, Greek or Sanskrit—had a word for chile peppers because no one in Europe, Africa, or Asia had ever seen these vegetables. Columbus sailed west in an attempt to find the fabled spice islands and that expensive spice, black pepper. Instead he found the islands of the Caribbean and an altogether new spice, which he called pepper, since that is what he was seeking.

When the conquistadors invaded Meso-america, they learned the Nahuatl name for the plant, chilli. And so, at last, Western Europeans had the name for this pungent new vegetable—the chile pepper. Peppers were adopted so thoroughly by the Old World that they now are the basis for the distinctive tastes of several cultures—the curry of India, the goulash of Hungary, the pepperoni of Italy, and the Szechuan dishes of central China.

Despite the enthusiastic adoption of chile peppers by warm climate cultures, most of Western Europe resisted this new vegetable, growing it only as a garden ornamental. Not until the early 1800s did the pepper gain acceptance in Western Europe, and the reason was Napoleon. As part of the military campaign to expand his empire, Napoleon had blockaded most ports, and spices became scarce. Suddenly the chile was "rediscovered" by Western Europeans and used as a substitute for more traditional seasonings.

Peppers came very late to the lands north of Mexico in the Western Hemisphere. Not until the southern United States was settled with plantations, and planters realized the climate was hospitable to growth of this flavorful plant, did peppers enter the American diet. This vegetable had been taken from South and Central America, across the ocean to Europe, and then 300 years later, brought back across the ocean to North America.

Bell peppers are so bland that little folklore has developed around them. The hotter peppers have long been thought to have medicinal value. The Incans believed peppers to be good for vision and able to repel poisonous snakes. The ancient wisdom is supported by today's scientific knowledge, for peppers are a rich source of beta-carotene which is, indeed, important for healthy eyes. As for repelling noxious animals, current organic gardening guides recommend using a pepper-water spray on your plants to discourage pests such as insects and rabbits.

Natives in old Mexico mixed peppers with garlic, oregano, and water to make an antacid. Early Mexicans also used the pepper to treat sore throats, rheumatism, and tumors. Even today, according to author Arturo Lomeli, "Chile…is the king, the soul of the Mexicans—a nutrient, a medicine, a drug, a comfort."

Incas worshiped the chile pepper as one of the four brothers in their creation myth, and they used peppers as currency. Pepper plants appear in the stone carvings on pre-Columbian monuments in Peru and in Oaxaca, Mexico.

Peppers are available in an exceptional range of colors and flavors. There are five basic forms of cultivated peppers, only two of which are well-known to North Americans: capsicum annuum, from which we get the bell or sweet pepper, the cayenne, and the fiery jalapeño; and capsicum frutescens, which produces the Tabasco pepper. From these two groups of peppers come green, red, and yellow peppers; big and small peppers; mild and fiery peppers. Chile peppers are rated for hotness on a Heat Scale that ranges from 1 (not hot) to 10 (wow!). The familiar green bell pepper rates only a 1 or 2, while the habanero, the hottest chile pepper, is a scorching 10. The jalapeño, used in our Hot Ice Cream, page 109, ranks in the middle of the scale with a heat value of 5.

SEASON AND QUALITY

Sweet bell peppers (red, yellow, and green) are available in supermarkets year-round, but the peak supply (and best price) is during the summer. Hot peppers are generally available all year as well, coming to northern markets from Mexico and year-round cultivation in the warm southern U.S. states.

Whatever type of pepper—hot or mild—you are buying, look for firm, glossy pods. Avoid peppers with wrinkled skins or soft spots. Bell peppers are sharpest when green and sweetest when they have turned red.

Store whole, fresh peppers in the vegetable drawer of the refrigerator for up to a week. Storage in a plastic bag will help to retain moisture, although too much moisture will cause the pepper to mold and spoil quickly. Hot peppers will keep longer in the refrigerator than will sweet peppers—for up to three weeks.

TIP: When preparing a hot pepper such as the jalapeño, be careful not to touch your face and be certain to wash your hands thoroughly afterwards. The seeds, skin, and flesh of this vegetable can cause a fierce burn to sensitive areas such as your eyes.

NUTRITIONAL QUALITY

Peppers are powerhouses of vitamins A and C. Surprisingly, a green bell pepper has twice as much vitamin C as does an equal weight of a fresh orange. And red bell peppers have more vitamin C than do the green peppers. Hot peppers are even richer sources of vitamin C than their mild, sweet bell pepper cousins. On an equal weight basis, hot peppers have more than 350% more vitamin C than do citrus fruits. (Of course, most people can't eat as much hot pepper as they can drink orange juice!)

For beta-carotene the story is the same. Red peppers are higher in the vitamin A precursor than are green peppers, and hot peppers are highest of all. One whole green bell pepper provides about 9% of the Daily Value for vitamin A; one sweet red pepper provides 84% of the Daily Value for vitamin A.

The compound in peppers that makes them hot is capsaicin. Bell peppers are mild because they contain very little capsaicin. This substance is usually concentrated in the seeds and white membrane rather than in the flesh of the pepper pod. There is no evidence that capsaicin causes ulcers, damages the linings of the intestinal tract, or causes or aggravates hemorrhoids. To the contrary, recent research suggests that capsaicin may help prevent cardiovascular disease by working as an anticoagulant. As vegetables rich in the antioxidant vitamins C and A, peppers may also help reduce risk of cancer.

Hot Ice Cream

The hot pepper and refreshing lime make this ice cream sparkle on your tongue. It's important to use a high quality premium French vanilla ice cream as the base. Since you'll eat small servings, the expense is not great.

8 SERVINGS

1 quart French vanilla ice cream   *1 1/2 teaspoons grated lime peel*
1 fresh jalapeño pepper

Let ice cream sit at room temperature 5 minutes to soften. While ice cream is softening, wash jalapeño pepper. Remove and discard seeds. Chop pepper finely. Stir pepper and lime peel into softened ice cream and either serve immediately or return to freezer until firm. Hot flavor increases after a few days in the freezer. Makes 1 quart.

Nutrition Facts (per serving)

Serving size 1/2 cup (80g); Servings per recipe 8; Calories 175; Calories from Fat 108; Total Fat 12g (18% DV); Saturated Fat 7g (35% DV); Cholesterol 45mg (15% DV); Vitamin A 21% DV; Vitamin C 24% DV; Sodium 55mg (2% DV); Total Carbohydrate 17g (6% DV); Dietary Fiber 0; Protein 2g, Calcium 8% DV; Iron 1% DV

Habanero Surprise

Invite your friends over to try a hot new recipe, but don't tell them what's in it!

24 SERVINGS

2/3 cup chopped sun-dried tomatoes

Nonstick vegetable cooking spray

1 habanero pepper, seeded, finely chopped*

Orange juice to replace the amount of water listed on cake mix package, minus 1/3 cup

18-ounce package yellow cake mix

3/4 cup pureed great northern beans

2 eggs

1/4 teaspoon almond extract

1/2 cup sunflower kernels, raw or roasted

Orange Frosting (recipe follows)

Preheat oven to 350°. To soften tomatoes, pour boiling water over tomatoes and let sit 5 minutes. Drain and chop.

Spray a 9-inch x 13-inch cake pan with cooking spray and set aside. Put tomatoes and habanero pepper in orange juice and allow to sit while mixing other ingredients. Combine cake mix, beans, eggs, and almond extract and beat for 2 minutes. Stir in juice/tomato/pepper mixture. Mix thoroughly. Fold in sunflower kernels and pour into prepared pan. Bake for 40 to 45 minutes. Cake is done when a toothpick inserted in center comes out clean. Cool on rack and frost with Orange Frosting.

*TIP: If you like hot food, include seeds and webbing of pepper.

Orange Frosting

2 cups powdered sugar, sifted

3 tablespoons margarine

2 tablespoons orange juice

1 tablespoon lemon juice

1 teaspoon orange extract

Cream powdered sugar and margarine with electric mixer until well blended; add juices and extract and beat to a smooth spreading consistency. If frosting is too thick, add milk or orange juice 1 teaspoon at a time.

Nutrition Facts (per serving)

Serving size 1 piece (60g); Servings per recipe 24; Calories 150; Calories from Fat 36; Total Fat 4g (6% DV); Saturated Fat 1g (5% DV); Cholesterol 23mg (8% DV); Vitamin A 2% DV; Vitamin C 17% DV; Sodium 195mg (8% DV); Total Carbohydrate 30g (10% DV); Dietary Fiber 1g (4% DV); Protein 3g; Calcium 5% DV; Iron 7% DV

Peppered Cocoa Cake

A hint of the southwest for all the Tex-Mex lovers.

24 SERVINGS

Nonstick vegetable cooking spray

1 1/2 cups sugar

3/4 cup oil

2 eggs

1/2 teaspoon almond flavoring

1 3/4 cups lentil puree (see page XXI)

1 cup mashed potatoes

1 cup all-purpose flour, sifted

6 tablespoons unsweetened cocoa

1 1/2 teaspoons baking soda

1/2 teaspoon salt

1/4 cup green bell pepper, diced fine

1/4 cup yellow bell pepper, diced fine

1/4 cup red bell pepper, diced fine

1 tablespoon minced fresh jalapeño
  pepper

Chocolate Almond Frosting (recipe
  below)

Preheat oven to 350°. Spray a 9-inch x 13-inch pan with cooking spray; set aside. (For an elegant layer cake, two 9-inch round pans can be used.) Beat sugar, oil, and eggs for 2 minutes. Add almond flavoring, lentil puree, and potatoes to the creamed mixture. Add flour, cocoa, soda, and salt to the mixture and beat for 2 minutes. Fold in the remaining four vegetables. Pour into prepared cake pan. Bake for 30 to 35 minutes. Cool and frost with Chocolate Almond Frosting.

TIP: May use 3/4 cup red or yellow peppers or a combination of both.

Chocolate Almond Frosting

9 tablespoons cocoa

2 cups powdered sugar, sifted

1/4 teaspoon salt

1/3 cup margarine, room temperature

3 tablespoons skim milk

1/2 teaspoon almond flavoring

1/2 cup sliced almonds

Sift first three ingredients into a large bowl. Add margarine and blend with a fork or pastry blender until mixture is like coarse meal. Add milk and beat until smooth. Stir in flavoring. Frost cake and then sprinkle with almonds. (If making a 9-inch layer cake, 1 1/2 recipes of frosting are needed to frost between layers and cover top and sides.)

Nutrition Facts (per serving)

Serving size 1 piece (75g); Servings per recipe 24; Calories 235; Calories from Fat 108; Total Fat 12g (18% DV); Saturated Fat 2g (10% DV); Cholesterol 23mg (8% DV); Vitamin A 3% DV; Vitamin C 6% DV; Sodium 155mg (7% DV); Total Carbohydrate 32g (11% DV); Dietary Fiber 2g (8% DV); Protein 4g; Calcium 2% DV; Iron 6% DV

Potatoes

"But don't forget the potatoes."—John Tyler Petee, *Prayer and Potatoes*

HISTORY

Like so many of our other favorite vegetables, the potato probably originated in the Western Hemisphere. When the Spanish explorers arrived in Peru, they found Incas who had been cultivating and enjoying the potato for nearly 2,000 years. The explorers returned to Europe with the new food, but acceptance was slow. Because it grew underground, the potato was seen as mysterious, evil, and poisonous. Sir Walter Raleigh recognized the potential of potatoes and helped to change their image. He was so successful that within less than 200 years the potato was the staple food of the Irish and was prominent in the German diet, too.

In France, the potato became popular through the efforts of a pharmacist, Antoine-Auguste Parmentier. An amusing anecdote shows that Parmentier was an early genius of marketing strategy. He persuaded Louis XVI to allow him to plant a large field of potatoes just outside Paris and to post prominent guards to protect the field. Their curiosity aroused, Parisians soon plundered the crop and potatoes were instantly chic. Parmentier's next step was to organize a lavish dinner for the royal court in which every course included potatoes. In honor of the creative thinking of the French pharmacist, French menus often bear the name Parmentier on potato dishes.

Today the potato is considered the fourth most important food crop in the world (after corn, wheat, and rice). Russia, Poland, and Germany lead the world in potato consumption (262 pounds per person per year), closely followed by Holland, Cyprus, Ireland, Belgium, Denmark, and Spain. Americans eat over 120 pounds of potatoes per person per year, making this the single most popular vegetable in the country.

The potato is favored by famous and non-famous alike. The favorite food of the French impressionist artist Paul Cezanne was potatoes sautéed in olive oil. And the author of *Winnie the Pooh*, A. A. Milne, said, "If a man really likes potatoes, he must be a pretty decent sort of fellow."

The nickname "spud" comes from Scotland, where potatoes were lifted from the soil using a three-pronged fork known as a spud.

Any food as important as the potato is sure to inspire folklore. The potato has been falsely blamed for causing leprosy, syphilis, tuberculosis, and flatulence. Thus, it is only fair that the potato has also been falsely credited with aphrodisiacal qualities.

Here are some folk remedies using the potato. To cure toothache, carry a potato in a pocket on the same side as the aching tooth. As the potato dries, the toothache will subside. Soothe a sunburn with a slice of raw potato. In like manner, a slice of raw potato will soothe eyes and erase the telltale signs of crying. A dried potato worn in a pouch on a necklace will cure rheumatism.

SEASON

The new crop appears each year from May through October. But potatoes are in season all year because they are superb keepers.

QUALITY AND STORAGE

The best potatoes are clean, uniform in size, smooth skinned, and free from bruises, cuts, and sprouts. A green coloration in the skin is solanine, a toxic chemical produced by exposure to light. Cut away the green skin. The rest of the potato is safe to eat. Sprouts are another problem. They are mildly toxic, too. Remove sprouts when preparing the potatoes, even cutting into the flesh a bit to completely remove the sprout.

To keep potatoes at peak quality, store in a cool, humid place away from light. You can store potatoes in the refrigerator or in a cupboard. Potatoes will last longest if kept at around 45 to 50 degrees and well ventilated. If the air is too dry, the potatoes will shrivel. If the air is too moist, the potatoes will rot.

NUTRITIONAL QUALITY

Despite popular belief, potatoes are low in calories. A whole medium potato has only 100 calories, about the same as a glass of 2% milk or one pear. Potatoes only become high-calorie foods when high-fat ingredients are added. It's what we put on them or what we cook them in that increases the calories, not the potato itself.

3 1/2 OUNCES OF POTATO	CALORIES	FAT GRAMS	FIBER GRAMS
Baked, with skin	100	0	2
Baked, with 2 tablespoons sour cream	248	6	2
French fries	315	17	1
Potato chips	525	35	1

Everyone knows potatoes are high in carbohydrates, but not everyone knows that the potato also has some valuable protein, 7% of the Daily Value for iron (a nutrient that is difficult to get), 50% of the Daily Value for vitamin C, and nearly 3 grams of dietary fiber (if you eat the skin). All this in a food that is fat free, cholesterol free, and very low in sodium. As an extra bonus, the potato is an excellent source of potassium and contains a valuable amount of vitamin B-6.

For more desserts using potatoes, see Chewy Garbanzo Spice Bars, page 12 ; Chocolate Surprise Cake, page 29 ; Danish Carrot Pudding, page 36; and Cocoa Lentil Cake with Cocoa Mocha Frosting, page 80.

Potato Candy Easter Eggs

Create an Easter tradition. A few days before Easter, gather friends and family to mix and shape the eggs. They are very rich, so you will have plenty to share.

36 MEDIUM EGGS

1/2 cup warm mashed potatoes

1/2 teaspoon salt

1/4 pound butter at room temperature; don't substitute margarine

2 pounds powdered sugar (7 cups)

12 ounces chocolate chips

Blend potatoes, salt, and butter. Add powdered sugar and stir until stiff. Transfer dough from bowl to a board thickly dusted with powdered sugar. Knead the dough well until it has a smooth, creamy consistency. Divide into four portions and flavor each as desired. Each portion will yield 9 eggs.

PEPPERMINT: few drops peppermint extract, green food coloring

COCONUT:　　1/2 cup coconut, pink food coloring

MAPLE NUT:　few drops maple flavor extract, 2 tablespoons chopped nuts

CHOCOLATE: 2 tablespoons cocoa, 2 tablespoons chopped nuts

ORANGE:　　1/4 teaspoon orange extract, orange food coloring

LEMON:　　　1/4 teaspoon lemon extract, yellow food coloring

VANILLA:　　1/2 teaspoon vanilla extract

Shape into egg shapes and size as desired. Chill in refrigerator several hours.

Roll in melted chocolate chips to cover. Chill again. Decorate tops with icing flowers and leaves if desired.

Nutrition Facts (per serving)

Serving size 1 medium egg (31g); Servings per recipe 36; Calories 120; Calories from Fat 27; Total Fat 3g (5% DV); Saturated Fat 2g (10% DV); Cholesterol 7mg (2% DV); Vitamin A 2% DV; Vitamin C 0; Sodium 65mg (3% DV); Total Carbohydrate 26g (9% DV); Dietary Fiber 1g (4% DV); Protein 0; Calcium 0; Iron 0

Potato Fudge

Adapted from a pioneer recipe, a sweet bit of heritage.

36 SERVINGS

Nonstick vegetable cooking spray

1/2 to 2/3 cup warm mashed potatoes
unseasoned (about 2 medium)

1/4 teaspoon salt

1 teaspoon vanilla extract

1 pound powdered sugar, sifted
(3 1/2 cups)

1/2 cup shredded coconut

1 ounce square unsweetened chocolate

2 teaspoons butter or margarine

Spray an 8-inch square pan with cooking spray; set in refrigerator to chill. Combine potatoes, salt, and vanilla in mixing bowl. Stir in some of the sugar—mixture will liquefy. Continue stirring in sugar until mixture is the consistency of fudge, about like a stiff dough. Knead it until it thickens. Add more sugar if necessary. Add coconut and spread evenly in pan. Melt chocolate and butter together; stir until evenly mixed. Spread over fudge. Cut into 36 pieces (6 by 6).

Nutrition Facts (per serving)

Serving size 1 square (20g); Servings per recipe 36; Calories 65; Calories from Fat 9; Total Fat 1g (1% DV); Saturated Fat 1g (5% DV); Cholesterol 1mg (0% DV); Vitamin A 0; Vitamin C 1% DV; Sodium 20mg (1% DV); Total Carbohydrate 14g (5% DV); Dietary Fiber 0; Protein 0; Calcium 0; Iron 1% DV

New Age Custard Pie

A delicate flavor as expected in a custard pie.

8 SERVINGS

1 cup sugar	1 cup evaporated skim milk
1 tablespoon butter flavoring	Juice of 1 lemon
3 eggs	9-inch deep-dish unbaked pastry
2 teaspoons vanilla flavoring	shell, homemade, frozen, or
2 medium potatoes	refrigerated

Preheat oven to 425°. Combine sugar, butter flavoring, eggs, and vanilla in a medium bowl, and beat with an electric mixer until fluffy. Set aside. Peel the potatoes and grate finely into the milk; fold into egg mixture. Add lemon juice. Pour into pastry shell and bake for 10 minutes; reduce heat to 325° and bake 30 minutes longer or until a knife inserted halfway between the center and edge comes out clean. Cool on rack.

Nutrition Facts (per serving)

Serving size 1 slice (140g); Servings per recipe 8; Calories 295; Calories from Fat 90; Total Fat 10g (15% DV); Saturated Fat 2g (10% DV); Cholesterol 104mg (35% DV); Vitamin A 4% DV; Vitamin C 12% DV; Sodium 200mg (8% DV); Total Carbohydrate 45g (15% DV); Dietary Fiber 1g (4% DV); Protein 7g; Calcium 11% DV; Iron 6% DV

All-American Chocolate Layer Cake

A great way to use leftover mashed potatoes.

16 SERVINGS

Nonstick vegetable cooking spray
2 cups all-purpose flour
2 teaspoons baking powder
1/2 teaspoon cinnamon
1/2 teaspoon cloves
1/2 teaspoon allspice
1/2 teaspoon nutmeg
9 tablespoons unsweetened cocoa

1 cup mashed potatoes
3 eggs, separated
2 cups sugar
1 cup prune puree (recipe page 195)
1 cup sliced almonds
Chocolate Frosting (recipe below)
Grated coconut

Preheat oven to 350°. Spray two 8-inch layer cake pans with cooking spray and dust lightly with flour; set aside. Sift flour with baking powder, spices, and cocoa; set aside. Put potatoes in a large bowl and beat in egg yolks, sugar, and prune puree. Mix until well blended. Fold flour mixture into batter. Beat egg whites to a stiff peak. Gently fold egg whites and almonds into potato batter, being careful not to overmix. Pour into pans and bake for 25 to 30 minutes or until toothpick inserted in center comes out clean. Spread Chocolate Frosting between layers, then on top and sides. Sprinkle with grated coconut.

Chocolate Frosting

9 tablespoons cocoa
1/3 cup margarine, room temperature
1/4 teaspoon salt

2 cups powdered sugar, sifted
1/2 teaspoon vanilla extract
3 tablespoons skim milk

In a medium bowl, blend first four ingredients. When well mixed, add vanilla and milk. If frosting is too stiff to spread easily, add additional milk 1 or 2 teaspoons at a time.

Nutrition Facts (per serving)

Serving size 1 piece (125g); Servings per recipe 16; Calories 390; Calories from Fat 90; Total Fat 10g (15% DV); Saturated Fat 2g (10% DV); Cholesterol 52mg (17% DV); Vitamin A 15% DV; Vitamin C 3% DV; Sodium 175mg (7% DV); Total Carbohydrate 75g (25% DV); Dietary Fiber 5g (20% DV); Protein 6g; Calcium 7% DV; Iron 14% DV

Irish Cake

Reminiscent of steamed pudding, but not as rich nor as long in the making.

12 SERVINGS

Nonstick vegetable cooking spray	1/4 cup unsweetened cocoa
1/2 cup margarine, softened	1/2 teaspoon cloves
1 cup sugar	1/2 teaspoon cinnamon
1/2 cup mashed potatoes	1/2 teaspoon nutmeg
2 eggs, beaten	1/2 cup wheat germ
3/4 cup crushed pineapple and juice	1/2 cup pecans
1/2 cup plain nonfat yogurt	Orange-Lemon Sauce (recipe below)
1 1/2 cups all-purpose flour	

Preheat oven to 350°. Spray a 6-cup turban mold or tube pan with cooking spray; dust with flour. Cream margarine and sugar; add mashed potatoes and eggs. Stir in pineapple, juice, and yogurt. Stir dry ingredients together and add slowly. Add pecans. Mix until thoroughly blended. Pour into prepared pan. Bake for 25 to 30 minutes or until cake tester comes out clean. Serve warm with Orange-Lemon Sauce. Individual servings can be warmed in the microwave and then served.

Orange-Lemon Sauce

1 cup orange juice	2/3 cup water
1/4 cup lemon juice	Artificial sweetener equal to
2 tablespoons cornstarch	1 cup sugar

Combine first four ingredients and cook over medium heat, stirring constantly. Bring to a boil and cook for 1 minute after mixture comes to a boil. Remove from heat and cool slightly. Stir in sweetener.

Nutrition Facts (per serving)

Serving size 1 slice (155g); Servings per recipe 12; Calories 295; Calories from Fat 108; Total Fat 12g (18% DV); Saturated Fat 2g (10% DV); Cholesterol 45mg (15% DV); Vitamin A 14% DV; Vitamin C 30% DV; Sodium 190mg (8% DV); Total Carbohydrate 44g (15% DV); Dietary Fiber 3g (12% DV); Protein 6g; Calcium 4% DV; Iron 13% DV

Pumpkin

HISTORY

The pumpkin is one of the great food gifts from the ancient Americas. Cultivated by pre-Columbian residents of the Western Hemisphere, pumpkins, once introduced to the European explorers, quickly became popular in Europe. Often confused with winter squashes, pumpkins grow on vines, while squashes grow on bushy plants.

While Americans generally think of pumpkin as little more than a Halloween decoration and a Thanksgiving dessert ingredient, this deep orange globe is enjoyed in the Orient as a vegetable in and of itself. In fact, there is an old legend from the East Indies that features a very large pumpkin indeed.

A certain nobleman had two things in his life that he loved dearly and of which he was inordinately proud—his only son and a grand pumpkin that he had carefully tended in his garden until it had reached a prodigious size. One sad day, the dearly loved son grew ill and died. The grief-stricken father couldn't bear to put his little son in an ordinary casket; and so, to show his great love, he decided to put his son's body into the prized pumpkin.

The father cut off the top and scooped out most of the seeds, leaving some flesh and some watery juice and seeds in case the boy's spirit should grow hungry and thirsty. The unique coffin was transported to a nearby mountain and gently placed under a pine tree. Two days later the father decided to bid his final farewell to his son. He walked up the mountain and lifted the top off the pumpkin. To his surprise he found it filled with water and swimming fishes and a whale.

Frightened and confused, the father fled to the nearest house and told the strange tale. Overhearing him, some boys thought they saw an easy way to catch fish for supper, and they decided to carry the pumpkin off to their own yard as a private fishing pond. Just as they tried to lift it, the distraught father came back. Frightened and a little guilty, the boys dropped the heavy pumpkin, which burst. The water and fishes flooded the land. The fishes, which had been the seeds, swam off to the sea and the whale, which was the old man's son, was never seen again.

A familiar children's tale features another gigantic pumpkin. We remember Cinderella, who went to the ball in a glittering, magic coach, transformed from the lowly garden pumpkin.

Pumpkins are naturally sweet and have a long tradition as an autumn dessert ingredient. John Greenleaf Whittier, a 19th century American poet, wrote lovingly of the pumpkin as a symbol of the autumn harvest and of warm family traditions.

THE PUMPKIN

Ah! On Thanksgiving Day, when from East and from West

From North and from South come the pilgrim and guest,

When the gray-haired New England sees round his board

The old broken links of affection restored,

When the care-wearied man seeks his mother once more,

And the worn matron smiles where the girl smiled before,

What moistens the lip and what brightens the eye?

What calls back the past like the rich Pumpkin Pie?

Oh—fruit loved of boyhood—the old days recalling,

When woodgrapes were purpling and brown nuts were falling!

When wild, ugly faces we carved in its skin,

Glaring out through the dark with a candle within!

When we laughed round the corn-heap, with hearts all in tune,

Our chair a broad pumpkin, our lantern the moon,

Telling tales of a fairy who traveled like steam,

In a pumpkin-shell coach, with two rats for her team!

SEASON

Whole, fresh pumpkins are available for a short season in late autumn—October and November. Fortunately, they are wonderful keepers, so the season can be extended for several months with proper storage. Canned pumpkin is a convenient way to enjoy pumpkin all year. In fact, canned pumpkin is made from a small, sweet, fleshy variety and is often better in recipes than fresh pumpkin.

QUALITY AND STORAGE

While nearly all fresh, whole pumpkins can be used for cooking, the small pie pumpkin has a sweeter flesh than does the large carving pumpkin.

Choose fresh pumpkins that are fully ripe, with firm rinds, bright orange color, and heavy weight. Watch out for soft spots or cracks that will decay rapidly. The deeper the orange color, the higher the carotene content.

Store in a cool, dry place away from frost danger. Uncut, pumpkins will store well for up to three months. Check them often, though, for they will suddenly start to rot and leak on the bottom without much visible warning.

NUTRITIONAL QUALITY

Pumpkins are one of the superstar vegetables, very rich in nutritional value. Because pure beta-carotene is deep orange, this color is a visual marker of carotene content, and carotenes are converted into vitamin A in your body. The deeper the color, the more generous the amount of the nutrient. One cup of cooked pumpkin provides over 1,000% of the Daily Value for Vitamin A! This is a high-potency vegetable! One cup of cooked pumpkin also provides 17% of the Daily Value for vitamin C, 15% of the Daily Value for folate, 6% of the Daily Value for calcium, and 19% of the Daily Value for iron. In addition to all this goodness, pumpkin is a good source of dietary fiber. One cup of the cooked vegetable con tains 11% of your Daily Value for fiber.

For an additional dessert incorporating pumpkin, see Pumpkin Tofu Pie, page 18.

Crisp Pumpkin Cookies

*A thin refrigerator cookie. Make up the dough ahead and bake
cookies as you want them — warm, fragrant, and fresh from the oven.*

9 DOZEN

Nonstick vegetable cooking spray

2 cups sugar

1 cup applesauce

2 eggs, beaten

4 cups sifted all-purpose flour

2 cups whole wheat flour

1/4 teaspoon salt

1 teaspoon baking soda

3 tablespoons pumpkin pie spice

*2 cups canned or thick-cooked
  pumpkin*

1 cup chopped nuts

Using an electric mixer, blend sugar and applesauce; add eggs. In a separate bowl, stir together flours, salt, soda, and spice; mix dry ingredients into creamed mixture alternately with the pumpkin. Add nuts. Form into two logs, wrap in waxed paper, and chill thoroughly in refrigerator until dough is stiff. (This will be several hours or overnight.)

Preheat oven to 375°. Spray baking sheets with cooking spray. Slice dough thin, about 1/8 inch, and bake for 10 to 12 minutes. Remove promptly to cooling rack. Cookies will be thin, light, and crisp. Browning is not easily seen.

Nutrition Facts (per serving)

Serving size 1 cookie (20g); Servings per recipe 108; Calories 50; Calories from Fat 9; Total Fat 1g (2% DV); Saturated Fat 0; Cholesterol 5mg (2% DV); Vitamin A 20% DV; Vitamin C 1% DV; Sodium 14mg (1% DV); Total Carbohydrate 10g (3% DV); Dietary Fiber 1g (4% DV); Protein 1g; Calcium 1% DV; Iron 3% DV

Pumpkin Nut Cookies

*Your family will love these and won't even realize the great
nutrition they're getting. Wonderful with either maple or lemon icing.*

4 DOZEN

Nonstick vegetable cooking spray	1/2 teaspoon salt
1/2 cup vegetable shortening	2 1/2 teaspoons cinnamon
1 cup sugar	1/2 teaspoon nutmeg
2 eggs	1/4 teaspoon ginger
1 cup canned pumpkin	1 cup chopped nuts
2 cups all-purpose flour	Quick Maple or Lemon Icing
4 teaspoons baking powder	(recipes below)

Preheat oven to 350°. Spray cookie sheets with cooking spray and set aside. Cream shortening and sugar; add eggs and pumpkin, and mix well. In a separate bowl mix flour, baking powder, salt, cinnamon, nutmeg, and ginger. Add dry ingredients to pumpkin mixture and mix until blended. Stir in nuts. Drop by teaspoonfuls onto prepared sheet. Bake for 15 minutes. When cool, frost with Quick Maple or Lemon Icing.

Quick Maple Icing

3 tablespoons margarine	1 teaspoon maple flavoring
2 cups sifted powdered sugar	3 tablespoons skim milk

In a medium bowl, mix margarine and powdered sugar. Add flavoring and milk and beat until frosting is uniformly smooth and creamy for easy spreading. If more milk is needed add one or two teaspoons at a time.

Lemon Icing

1 1/2 cups powdered sugar	5 teaspoons skim milk
2 tablespoons margarine	3/4 teaspoon lemon extract

In a medium bowl, beat all ingredients together until smooth.

Nutrition Facts (per serving)

Serving size 1 cookie (26g); Servings per recipe 48; Calories 92; Calories from Fat 36; Total Fat 4g (6% DV); Saturated Fat 1g (5% DV); Cholesterol 11mg (4% DV); Vitamin A 23% DV; Vitamin C 1% DV; Sodium 60mg (2% DV); Total Carbohydrate 12g (4% DV); Dietary Fiber 0; Protein 1g; Calcium 1% DV; Iron 3% DV

Chocolate Chip Pumpkin Cookies

Surprisingly, chocolate chips and pumpkin go together exceptionally well.

5 1/2 DOZEN

Nonstick vegetable cooking spray

2 1/4 cups all-purpose flour

1 teaspoon baking powder

1/2 teaspoon baking soda

1/2 teaspoon salt

1 1/2 teaspoons pumpkin pie spice

1 cup margarine, softened

1 cup sugar

15-ounce can solid pack pumpkin

2 eggs

1 teaspoon vanilla flavoring

2 cups semi-sweet chocolate chips

1 cup walnuts

Vanilla Glaze (recipe below)

Preheat oven to 375°. Spray cookie sheets with cooking spray; set aside. In a small bowl, combine flour, baking powder, baking soda, salt, and pumpkin pie spice; set aside. In a large mixer bowl, beat margarine and sugar until creamy. Add pumpkin, eggs, and vanilla. Gradually add flour mixture. Stir in chocolate chips and nuts. Drop cookies by level measuring tablespoonfuls onto prepared baking sheet. Bake for 18 to 20 minutes, until edges are lightly browned. Let stand 5 minutes. Remove from cookie sheets and cool. Combine glaze ingredients and spread on cookies.

Vanilla Glaze

1 cup powdered sugar, sifted

1 tablespoon skim milk

1/2 teaspoon vanilla extract

Combine ingredients and spread on cookies when they are cool.

Nutrition Facts (per serving)

Serving size 1 cookie (30g); Servings per recipe 66; Calories 100; Calories from Fat 54; Total Fat 6g (9% DV); Saturated Fat 2g (10% DV); Cholesterol 8mg (3% DV); Vitamin A 35% DV; Vitamin C 1% DV; Sodium 60mg (3% DV); Total Carbohydrate 12g (4% DV); Dietary Fiber 1g (4% DV); Protein 1g; Calcium 1% DV; Iron 3% DV.

Peter Pumpkin Squares

A great after school snack or finish to a meal. Chewy texture.

24 SERVINGS

Nonstick vegetable cooking spray	*1 1/2 cups all-purpose flour*
15-ounce can pumpkin	*1 1/2 cups quick-cooking oats*
1 1/2 cups brown sugar	*1 tablespoon cinnamon*
4 eggs	*2 teaspoons baking powder*
3/4 cup applesauce	*1 teaspoon baking soda*

Preheat oven to 350°. Spray a 9-inch x 13-inch pan with cooking spray and set aside. Combine pumpkin, brown sugar, eggs, and applesauce. Mix until well blended. Combine dry ingredients; add to pumpkin mixture and mix well. Pour into prepared pan and bake for 30 minutes. To test for doneness, insert toothpick in center. It should come out clean. When cool, cut into 24 squares (4 by 6).

Nutrition Facts (per serving)

Serving size 1 bar (64g); Servings per recipe 24; Calories 125; Calories from Fat 18; Total Fat 2g (3% DV); Saturated Fat 0; Cholesterol 45mg (16% DV); Vitamin A 91% DV; Vitamin C 2% DV; Sodium 80mg (4% DV); Total Carbohydrate 26g (8% DV); Dietary Fiber 1g (4% DV); Protein 3g; Calcium 3% DV; Iron 8% DV

Pumpkin Pie Squares

Truly just a little piece of pie.

12 SERVINGS

Crust

3/4 cup all-purpose flour

3/4 cup quick-cooking oats

1/2 cup brown sugar, packed

1/2 cup margarine, softened

Preheat oven to 350°. Combine all ingredients with an electric mixer at a low speed. Mix until crumbly. Pour into an ungreased 9-inch x 13-inch pan. Bake for 15 minutes. Meanwhile, prepare filling. Remove pan from oven and press dough onto bottom and sides to form crust.

Pumpkin Filling

2 cups canned pumpkin

2 1/3 cups evaporated skim milk

1 egg

3/4 cup sugar

3/4 cup brown sugar, packed

3/4 teaspoon salt

1 1/2 teaspoons cinnamon

3/4 teaspoon ginger

1/2 teaspoon cloves

Combine ingredients in mixing bowl and beat well. Pour into formed crust and bake at 350° for 50 minutes or until filling is set. Cut into 12 servings (4 by 3).

Nutrition Facts (per serving)

Serving size 1 square (150g); Servings per recipe 12; Calories 310; Calories from Fat 81; Total Fat 9g (14% DV); Saturated Fat 2g (10% DV); Cholesterol 25mg (8% DV); Vitamin A 191% DV; Vitamin C 4% DV; Sodium 295g (12% DV); Total Carbohydrate 53g (18% DV); Dietary Fiber 1g (4% DV); Protein 6g; Calcium 19% DV; Iron 11% DV

Kids' Pumpkin Butterscotch Pudding

Kid tested—dietitian approved! Let the kids make it.

8 SERVINGS

1 package instant, sugar-free
  butterscotch pudding mix
2 cups skim milk
15-ounce can pumpkin

1 teaspoon cinnamon*
1/2 teaspoon ginger
1/4 teaspoon nutmeg

Add pudding mix to milk in a large mixing bowl. Mix 30 seconds until blended. Blend in pumpkin and spices. Chill in refrigerator 2 hours.

*TIP: 1 teaspoon pumpkin pie spice can be used instead of the three spices listed.

Nutrition Facts (per serving)

Serving size 1/2 cup (130g); Servings per recipe 8; Calories 70; Calories from Fat 0; Total Fat 0; Saturated Fat 0 ; Cholesterol 0; Vitamin A 273% DV; Vitamin C 5% DV; Sodium 205mg (9% DV); Total Carbohydrate 10g (3% DV); Dietary Fiber 1g (4% DV); Protein 3g; Calcium 10% DV; Iron 5% DV

Halloween Ice Cream

Easy to make, great to taste, fun anytime you want pumpkin's flavor and nutrition.

8 SERVINGS

1/2 cup evaporated skim milk

1/4 cup honey

1 cup canned or thick cooked pumpkin

1/4 teaspoon cinnamon

1/4 teaspoon ginger

1/4 teaspoon nutmeg

1/4 teaspoon salt

3 cups low-fat whipped topping,
   thawed (8-ounce container)

Combine milk and honey in a saucepan and stir over medium heat until well blended and hot. Do not let the mixture boil. Stir in pumpkin, spices, and salt. Chill thoroughly. When cold, carefully fold in whipped topping. Pour into a shallow pan and freeze until solid.

Nutrition Facts (per serving)

Serving size 1/2 cup (65g); Servings per recipe 8; Calories 85; Calories from Fat 27; Total Fat 3g (5% DV); Saturated Fat 2g (10% DV); Cholesterol 1mg (0% DV); Vitamin A 138% DV; Vitamin C 3% DV; Sodium 90mg (4% DV); Total Carbohydrate 15g (5% DV); Dietary Fiber 0; Protein 2g; Calcium 6% DV; Iron 3% DV

Pumpkin Apple Fritters

So good you'll make them again and again.

20 SERVINGS

Oil for deep fat frying	2 cups applesauce
2 eggs, beaten	1 cup canned pumpkin
1/2 cup sugar	1/4 cup wheat germ
1 teaspoon cinnamon	1/2 teaspoon baking powder
2 teaspoons nutmeg	2 cups biscuit mix

Preheat oil to about 375°. Mix eggs, sugar, spices, applesauce, and pumpkin. Stir in wheat germ, followed by baking powder and biscuit mix. Do not beat. Drop batter by 1/4-cup amounts into hot oil. Cook about 4 minutes on each side. Serve warm.

Nutrition Facts (per serving)

Serving size 1 fritter (65g); Servings per recipe 20; Calories 135; Calories from Fat 54; Total Fat 6g (9% DV); Saturated Fat 1g (5% DV); Cholesterol 28mg (9% DV); Vitamin Λ 56% DV; Vitamin C 3% DV; Sodium 200g (8% DV); Total Carbohydrate 19g (6% DV); Dietary Fiber 1g (4% DV); Protein 2g; Calcium 1% DV; Iron 6% DV

Self-Crust Pumpkin Pie

This pie is super easy because it makes its own crust during baking.

8 SERVINGS

Nonstick vegetable cooking spray

2 eggs

2 cups canned or thick cooked pumpkin

1 cup nonfat dry milk powder

2/3 cup brown or white sugar

1/4 teaspoon salt

1 teaspoon cinnamon

1/2 teaspoon ginger

1/4 teaspoon nutmeg

1/4 cup whole wheat flour

1 cup water

Preheat oven to 350°. Spray a 9-inch pie plate with cooking spray; set aside. In a large mixing bowl, combine all ingredients except water; stir to mix. Add water gradually until well mixed. Pour into pie pan. Bake for 45 to 55 minutes or until a knife inserted halfway between edge and center comes out clean.

Nutrition Facts (per serving)

Serving size 1 wedge (200g); Servings per recipe 8; Calories 162; Calories from Fat 18; Total Fat 2g (3% DV); Saturated Fat 1g (5% DV); Cholesterol 70mg (23% DV); Vitamin A 276% DV; Vitamin C 5% DV; Sodium 135mg (6% DV); Total Carbohydrate 32g (11% DV); Dietary Fiber 2g (8% DV); Protein 6g; Calcium 13% DV; Iron 9% DV

Gingerbread in a Pumpkin Shell

Find a cute, squat pumpkin that will be baked into a spectacular dessert.

8 SERVINGS

Whole 3 pound squatty pie pumpkin

Nonstick vegetable cooking spray

1 teaspoon margarine

1 tablespoon brown sugar

14-ounce package gingerbread mix

Applesauce equal to liquid for
   cake mix

Low-fat whipped topping for garnish

Preheat oven to 350°. Wash pumpkin, pat dry, cut off top to create a wide opening, and clean out the seeds and pulp. (Reserve seeds if you wish to toast them for snacking.) Spray an 8-inch or 9-inch square pan with cooking spray and set pumpkin in pan for ease of handling. Put margarine and brown sugar in pumpkin shell and set in oven for 15 to 20 minutes. Occasionally during baking time, baste inside of pumpkin with margarine/sugar mixture.

Meanwhile, prepare gingerbread mix, substituting applesauce for the water or milk called for on the box. Pour batter into partially baked pumpkin shell, filling only to two-thirds capacity. (If there is extra batter, bake it in a custard cup or muffin tin.) Bake with top on or off , depending on how you wish to serve the dessert, in 350° oven until shell is tender and gingerbread tests done with a toothpick. Cooking time will be about one-half again as long as box mix states. To serve, cut pumpkin and cake into wedge-shaped slices and garnish with a dollop of whipped topping. Serve warm at the table so everyone can enjoy your clever creation.

Nutrition Facts (per serving)

Serving size 1 portion (220g); Servings per recipe 8; Calories 285; Calories from Fat 72; Total Fat 8g (12% DV); Saturated Fat 3g (15% DV); Cholesterol 0; Vitamin A 27% DV; Vitamin C 11% DV; Sodium 370mg (15% DV); Total Carbohydrate 50g (17% DV); Dietary Fiber 3g (12% DV); Protein 3g; Calcium 6% DV; Iron 14% DV

Pumpkin Splendor

*This simple jam-type filling can be spread on an English muffin
if you like and is also an ingredient in several of our recipes.*

3 CUPS

3/4 cup golden raisins, chopped

3/4 cup dried apricots, chopped

3/4 cup sugar

1/2 cup water

15-ounce can pumpkin or 1 3/4 to

2 cups pumpkin puree from

fresh pumpkin

Put raisins, apricots, sugar, and water in a medium saucepan and simmer 10 to 12 minutes, stirring occasionally. Add the pumpkin and mix thoroughly.

Nutrition Facts (per serving)

Serving size 1 tablespoon (20g); Servings per recipe 48; Calories 25; Calories from Fat 0; Total Fat 0; Saturated Fat 0; Cholesterol 0; Vitamin A 48% DV; Vitamin C 1% DV; Sodium 1mg (0% DV); Total Carbohydrate 7g (2% DV); Dietary Fiber 1g (4% DV); Protein 0; Calcium 0; Iron 2% DV

Thumbprint Cookies

A small batch of cookies that is just right for a small household.

30 COOKIES

Nonstick vegetable cooking spray

9-ounce package yellow cake mix

1/3 cup solid vegetable shortening

1 egg, separated

1 tablespoon skim milk

1 tablespoon water

3/4 cup oat bran

1/2 cup Pumpkin Splendor

(recipe page 134)

Preheat oven to 375°. Lightly spray cookie sheets with cooking spray; set aside. In a medium mixing bowl, combine cake mix, shortening, egg yolk, and milk. Mix well. Shape into 1-inch balls. Beat egg white and water slightly. Dip balls in egg mixture and roll in oat bran. Place 2 inches apart on cookie sheets. Press thumb into center of each ball to leave an indentation. Bake for 12 to 15 minutes or until set. Cool several minutes on cookie sheet, remove to rack and finish cooling. Fill each thumbprint with 1/2 teaspoon Pumpkin Splendor.

Nutrition Facts (per serving)

Serving size 1 cookie (12g); Servings per recipe 30; Calories 110; Calories from Fat 36; Total Fat 4g (6% DV); Saturated Fat 1g (5% DV); Cholesterol 9mg (3% DV); Vitamin A 13% DV; Vitamin C 0; Sodium 115mg (5% DV); Total Carbohydrate 18g (6% DV); Dietary Fiber 1g (4% DV); Protein 1g; Calcium 4% DV; Iron 3% DV

Amber Angel Bars

A delicious no-fat treat.

24 SERVINGS

*16-ounce package one-step angel
food cake mix*

*2 cups Pumpkin Splendor
(recipe page 134)*

Preheat oven to 350°. Combine the two ingredients, mixing well, and pour batter into an ungreased 10 1/2-inch x 15 1/2-inch jelly roll pan. Bake for 20 to 25 minutes. Cool and cut 4x6. Cover loosely with waxed paper for storage.

Nutrition Facts (per serving)

Serving size 1 bar (50g); Servings per recipe 24; Calories 100; Calories from Fat 0; Total Fat 0; Saturated Fat 0; Cholesterol 0; Vitamin A 64% DV; Vitamin C 1% DV; Sodium 135mg (6% DV); Total Carbohydrate 24g (8% DV); Dietary Fiber 1g (4% DV); Protein 2g; Calcium 3% DV; Iron 3% DV

Pumpkin Splendor Tartlets

A quick way to present an elegant tray of desserts.

16 SERVINGS

Pastry dough for a 2-crust pie
1 cup Pumpkin Splendor
(recipe page 134)

Low-fat whipped topping and
grated nutmeg for garnish

Preheat oven to 475°. You'll need a 3-inch fluted oval or round tartlet (3/4-inch deep) or mini-muffin pans. Roll pastry and outline a shape about half again the size of the baking tins. Shape pastry into pans and prick with fork. Bake for 5 minutes. Watch closely to prevent overbrowning.

When cool, remove tartlet crusts from tins and fill with Pumpkin Splendor. Garnish each tartlet with a small dot of low-fat whipped topping and a hint of grated nutmeg. Set on lacy doily on a serving plate.

Nutrition Facts (per serving)

Serving size 1 tartlet (40g); Servings per recipe 16; Calories 120; Calories from Fat 54; Total Fat 6g (9% DV); Saturated Fat 1g (5% DV); Cholesterol 0; Vitamin A 48% DV; Vitamin C 1% DV; Sodium 165mg (7% DV); Total Carbohydrate 16g (5% DV); Dietary Fiber 1g (4% DV); Protein 2g; Calcium 1% DV; Iron 5% DV

Mocha Fantasy

Wow them with this terrific dessert that is so easy to create.

12 SERVINGS

10-inch angel food cake
3 cups Pumpkin Splendor
(recipe page 134)
1 tablespoon instant coffee granules

3 cups low-fat frozen whipped
topping, thawed
1/3 cup sliced toasted almonds

If using a cake mix, prepare the angel food cake according to package directions and allow to cool. Split angel food cake into 3 layers using a serrated knife or dental floss. Put layers together using half of the Pumpkin Splendor between each layer. Fold coffee granules into whipped topping; spread over top and sides of cake. Sprinkle with toasted almonds. Chill until set—two to three hours. Slice with serrated knife.

Nutrition Facts (per serving)

Serving size 1 slice (135g); Servings per recipe 12; Calories 285; Calories from Fat 45; Total Fat 5g (8% DV); Saturated Fat 2g (10% DV); Cholesterol 0; Vitamin A 194% DV; Vitamin C 4% DV; Sodium 275mg (11% DV); Total Carbohydrate 59g (20% DV); Dietary Fiber 2g (8% DV); Protein 5g; Calcium 7% DV; Iron 8% DV

Marbled Pumpkin Cake

Take this to a potluck and listen to the praise.

24 SERVINGS

Cake

Nonstick vegetable cooking spray

2 1/4 cups all-purpose flour

2 teaspoons cinnamon

1 teaspoon baking soda

1/2 teaspoon salt

2 eggs

2 cups sugar

1 1/4 cups canned or thick cooked
  pumpkin

1/4 cup vegetable oil

1/2 teaspoon vanilla flavoring

Filling

8-ounce tub light cream cheese,
  room temperature

1 egg

1 tablespoon sugar

Topping

3/4 cup flaked coconut

1/2 cup chopped nuts

1/4 cup sugar

1/2 teaspoon cinnamon

Preheat oven to 350°. Spray a 9-inch x 13-inch cake pan with cooking spray; set aside. Combine flour, cinnamon, soda, and salt in large bowl. Set aside. Combine eggs, sugar, pumpkin, oil, and vanilla in small bowl; mix well. Add liquid mixture to flour mixture; stir just until moistened. Spread batter into prepared pan. Beat cream cheese, egg, and sugar thoroughly. Top cake batter with heaping teaspoons of filling. Swirl with knife to marbleize. Combine topping ingredients. Sprinkle evenly over batter. Bake for 30 to 35 minutes, or until a toothpick inserted in the center comes out clean. Cool on wire rack.

Nutrition Facts (per serving)

Serving size 1 piece (65g); Servings per recipe 24; Calories 200; Calories from Fat 63; Total Fat 7g (11% DV); Saturated Fat 3g (15% DV); Cholesterol 40mg (13% DV); Vitamin A 58% DV; Vitamin C 1% DV; Sodium 110mg (5% DV); Total Carbohydrate 30g (10% DV); Dietary Fiber 1g (4% DV); Protein 3g; Calcium 2% DV; Iron 6% DV

Pumpkin Plus Cheesecake

Invite the whole crowd; this dessert serves 14 people!

14 SERVINGS

Base

2 cups graham cracker crumbs

1/4 cup margarine, melted

1/4 cup sugar

1 teaspoon cinnamon

1/2 teaspoon nutmeg

1/4 teaspoon ginger

Combine ingredients in large bowl. Press mixture into bottom of a 10-inch springform pan. Set aside.

Filling

8-ounce tub light cream cheese,
room temperature

16 ounces firm tofu, cut in cubes

1 cup sugar

2 eggs

1 teaspoon vanilla flavoring

1 teaspoon cinnamon

1/2 teaspoon nutmeg

1/4 teaspoon ginger

1/4 teaspoon salt

3 tablespoons flour

2 cups canned or thick cooked
pumpkin

Low-fat whipped topping, thawed

Preheat oven to 350°. Combine light cream cheese and tofu in a large bowl. With an electric mixer, beat in sugar and then eggs one at a time. Add vanilla flavoring. Stir in spices and flour. When mixture is uniform, add pumpkin and blend thoroughly. Pour into springform pan. Bake for 90 minutes or until a toothpick inserted in center comes out clean. Turn off heat and let cake stay in oven an additional 30 minutes.

Remove from oven, cool, cover, and refrigerate overnight to allow flavors to mellow. Serve with a dollop of whipped topping. If desired, garnish with a toasted pecan half and a sprinkle of cinnamon or grated fresh nutmeg.

Nutrition Facts (per serving)

Serving size 1 piece (120g); Servings per recipe 14; Calories 235; Calories from Fat 90; Total Fat 10g (15% DV); Saturated Fat 4g (20% DV); Cholesterol 48mg (16% DV); Vitamin A 160% DV; Vitamin C 3% DV; Sodium 190mg (8% DV); Total Carbohydrate 33g (11% DV); Dietary Fiber 1g (4% DV); Protein 5g; Calcium 6% DV; Iron 10% DV

Pumpkin Butterscotch Snack Cakes

No frosting is needed for this quickly made treat.

24 SERVINGS

Nonstick vegetable cooking spray
2 1/2 cups all-purpose flour
1 tablespoon baking powder
1 teaspoon baking soda
1/2 teaspoon salt
2 teaspoons cinnamon
3/4 teaspoon nutmeg

15-ounce can pumpkin
4 eggs
1 1/2 cups packed brown sugar
1/2 cup vegetable oil
1 cup chopped walnuts, divided
2 cups (12-ounce package)
  butterscotch-flavored chips, divided

Preheat oven to 350°. Spray 24 muffin cups with cooking spray or line muffin cups with paper; set aside. Combine flour, baking powder, soda, salt, cinnamon, and nutmeg in medium bowl, set aside. In a large mixing bowl, beat pumpkin, eggs, brown sugar, and oil at medium speed for 3 minutes. Fold flour mixture into batter. Stir in 1/2 cup of the walnuts and 1 cup of the butterscotch chips. Combine remaining nuts and chips in a small bowl. Spoon 1/4 cup batter into each of the 24 muffin cups. Top with about 1 tablespoon of nut/chip mixture. Bake for 20 to 25 minutes or until wooden pick inserted in center comes out clean. Remove to wire rack to cool completely.

Nutrition Facts (per serving)

Serving size 1 cupcake (75g); Servings per recipe 24; Calories 190; Calories from Fat 108; Total Fat 12g (18% DV); Saturated Fat 4g (20% DV); Cholesterol 45mg (11% DV); Vitamin A 80% DV; Vitamin C 2% DV; Sodium 145mg (6% DV); Total Carbohydrate 34g (11% DV); Dietary Fiber 1g (4% DV); Protein 4g; Calcium 4% DV; Iron 8% DV

Golden Cupcakes

A quick and easy snack with a nutrition bonus.

24 CUPCAKES

1 1/2 cups whole wheat flour	3 eggs, slightly beaten
1 cup all-purpose flour	1 cup skim milk
3/4 cup sugar	1/2 cup vegetable oil
2 tablespoons baking powder	1 cup canned pumpkin
2 teaspoons cinnamon	3/4 cup golden raisins
1/2 teaspoon nutmeg	1 tablespoon vanilla flavoring
1/4 teaspoon salt	

Preheat oven to 350°. Place 24 paper baking cups in muffin tins. Stir together dry ingredients. Mix remaining ingredients and add to dry ingredients, stirring until barely moistened. Fill paper cups two-thirds full. Bake for 20 minutes or until toothpick inserted in center comes out clean. Remove from tins and cool on rack.

TIP: These cupcakes freeze exceptionally well.

Nutrition Facts (per serving)

Serving size 1 cupcake (55g); Servings per recipe 24; Calories 140; Calories from Fat 54; Total Fat 6g (9% DV); Saturated Fat 1g (5% DV); Cholesterol 35mg (12% DV); Vitamin A 46% DV; Vitamin C 1% DV; Sodium 120mg (5% DV); Total Carbohydrate 20g (7% DV); Dietary Fiber 1g (4% DV); Protein 3g; Calcium 4% DV; Iron 6% DV

Easy Pumpkin Cake

Frosting is not necessary, for there is plenty of flavor!

16 SERVINGS

Nonstick vegetable cooking spray

18-ounce package spice cake mix

1 cup mashed cooked or canned pumpkin

2 eggs

Water as stated on cake package,
minus 1/3 cup

1 teaspoon cinnamon

Preheat oven to 350°. Spray a 9-inch x 13-inch cake pan or a 9-inch tube pan with cooking spray; lightly flour; set aside. Combine dry cake mix, pumpkin, eggs, water, and cinnamon. Mix as directed on package. Pour the batter into prepared pan and bake for 40 to 45 minutes.

TIP: Canned or cooked mashed winter squash would also make a delicious cake.

Nutrition Facts (per serving)

Serving size 1 piece (95g); Servings per recipe 16; Calories 195; Calories from Fat 45; Total Fat 5g (8% DV); Saturated Fat 2g (10% DV); Cholesterol 35mg (12% DV); Vitamin A 68% DV; Vitamin C 1% DV; Sodium 310mg (13% DV); Total Carbohydrate 35g (12% DV); Dietary Fiber 1g (4% DV); Protein 3g; Calcium 11% DV; Iron 6% DV

Pumpkin Pudding Cake

Quick and easy, flavorful and nutritious; a novice will take pride in the results.

16 SERVINGS

29-ounce can pumpkin	1/2 teaspoon salt
12-ounce can evaporated skim milk	1/2 teaspoon ginger
3 eggs, beaten	1/2 teaspoon cloves
1 1/4 cups sugar	18-ounce yellow cake mix
2 teaspoons cinnamon	1 cup chopped walnuts
1 teaspoon nutmeg	1 cup boiling water

Preheat oven to 350°. Mix pumpkin, milk, eggs, sugar, cinnamon, nutmeg, salt, ginger, and cloves with an electric mixer until well blended. Pour pumpkin mixture into ungreased 9-inch x 13-inch pan. Sprinkle cake mix over pumpkin. Sprinkle walnuts over the cake mix and then carefully pour the boiling water evenly over the top of the pan. Bake for 50 to 60 minutes or until a sharp knife inserted 1 inch from edge comes out clean.

Nutrition Facts (per serving)

Serving size 1 piece (175g); Servings per recipe 16; Calories 295; Calories from Fat 72; Total Fat 8g (12% DV); Saturated Fat 1g (5% DV); Cholesterol 50mg (17% DV); Vitamin A 246% DV; Vitamin C 5% DV; Sodium 360mg (15% DV); Total Carbohydrate 52g (17% DV); Dietary Fiber 2g (8% DV); Protein 6g; Calcium 16% DV; Iron 10%

Rhubarb

HISTORY

Rhubarb is the vegetable that eats like a fruit. This wonderful, rosy, spring vegetable has been prized for centuries by those who live in northern climates. The
Chinese were the first to appreciate these tasty, thick stems. Carried by trading
caravans to the Volga River (long ago known as the Rha River), rhubarb then
traveled by boat down the river to the ancient civilizations of Greece and Rome.
Because the new vegetable came from the Rha and the "barbarians," the Romans
called it rhabarbum, from which we have our modern name, "rhubarb."

In 16th-century England, the leaves were used as a potent medication. Potent
indeed! Our modern knowledge has revealed that the leaves are toxic. Anyway,
one day a cook had stripped the leaves from the stalks and was boiling them for
medicinal use. The stalks were on the floor, ready to be thrown outside on the
garbage heap. He turned to make a pie for supper and discovered that he had no
fruit. What to do? He looked down at the stalks that he had not yet discarded.
Cautiously he tasted one. It was juicy but not sweet. He decided to experiment.
The resulting pie was so successful that rhubarb is called pie-plant to this day.

SEASON

Rhubarb is the first taste of spring, a welcome treat after winter. Rhubarb is harvested in hothouses from January through March, then in fields from April through June. Fresh rhubarb is available only in spring but frozen rhubarb is available year-round.

QUALITY AND STORAGE

High quality fresh rhubarb is firm, crisp, tender, and pink or red. Look for thick, young stalks, which generally are more tender. Colorful stalks usually have more flavor. Wilted, flabby stalks or pithy, rough, stringy stalks are past their prime. Field-grown rhubarb has a rich, dark red color, while hothouse rhubarb is light pink and milder in flavor.

Store whole, fresh rhubarb stalks in the coldest, moistest part of the refrigerator. Fresh rhubarb cut into 1-inch pieces can be stored in plastic bags in the refrigerator. The ends will split and curl but flavor and safety will be maintained. Either whole or cut rhubarb can be refrigerated safely for up to 2 weeks.

NUTRITIONAL QUALITY

One cup of fresh rhubarb chunks has less than 30 calories and nearly a gram of dietary fiber. Rhubarb is a fairly good source of calcium and an excellent source of potassium. One cup provides 17% of the RDA for vitamin C and 4% of the RDA for folate. Rhubarb is fat free.

Rhubarb Sherbet

A distinctive touch for an old favorite.

6 SERVINGS

2 cups rhubarb, diced	*1/4 cup cold water*
1 cup water	*1/16 teaspoon salt*
1/2 cup sugar	*1/3 cup orange marmalade*
2 teaspoons unflavored gelatin	*1 cup whipped topping, thawed*

In a medium saucepan, combine rhubarb, 1 cup water, and sugar. Cover and cook slowly until rhubarb is tender, about 3 to 4 minutes. Soften gelatin in 1/4 cup water a few minutes. Add to rhubarb. Stir until dissolved. Add salt. Cool. Add orange marmalade, and stir until blended. Pour into pan and freeze until partially frozen. Fold in whipped topping. Continue freezing until firm. Stir occasionally to prevent ice crystals forming.

Nutrition Facts (per serving)

Serving size 1/2 cup 80 (42g); Servings per recipe 6; Calories 185; Calories from Fat 27; Total Fat 3g (5% DV); Saturated Fat 3g (15% DV); Cholesterol 0; Vitamin A 3% DV; Vitamin C 4% DV; Sodium 30mg (1% DV); Total Carbohydrate 57g (19% DV); Dietary Fiber 1g (4% DV); Protein 2g; Calcium 5% DV; Iron 2% DV

Rhubarb Cream Pudding

An elegant taste of spring!

6 SERVINGS

Nonstick vegetable cooking spray

1 cup plain, fat-free yogurt

1 cup sugar

1 egg, slightly beaten

1 1/2 cups sifted all-purpose flour

1/2 teaspoon baking soda

1/2 teaspoon baking powder

1/4 teaspoon salt

1/2 teaspoon vanilla flavoring

1/4 teaspoon almond extract

2 cups rhubarb, diced into 1/2-inch
  pieces

Preheat oven to 375°. Spray an 8-inch square pan with cooking spray; set aside. Mix yogurt and sugar in a large bowl; add egg and mix well. Sift flour, baking soda, baking powder, and salt into yogurt mixture. Add vanilla flavoring and almond extract. Stir until blended. Fold in rhubarb. Pour into prepared pan. Bake for 35 minutes or until knife inserted near center comes out clean. Serve warm.

Nutrition Facts (per serving)

Serving size 1 square (185g); Servings per recipe 6; Calories 320; Calories from Fat 18; Total Fat 2g (3% DV); Saturated Fat 1g (5% DV); Cholesterol 90mg (31% DV); Vitamin A 3% DV; Vitamin C 5% DV; Sodium 240mg (10% DV); Total Carbohydrate 69g (23% DV); Dietary Fiber 3g (12% DV); Protein 8g; Calcium 21% DV; Iron 11% DV

Almond Rhubarb Sauce

The subtle, unexpected almond flavoring will gain new rhubarb fans.
Add a drop of red food coloring to enhance the rosy glow.

4 SERVINGS

1 cup sugar	*4 cups rhubarb, cut into 1/2-inch pieces*
1/4 cup water	*1/2 teaspoon almond extract*

Bring sugar and water to boil. Add rhubarb; reduce heat. Cover and simmer for 5 minutes, or until tender. Remove from heat; stir in almond extract. Serve as is, or over low-fat vanilla ice cream or angel food cake.

Nutrition Facts (per serving)

Serving size 1/2 cup (200g); Servings per recipe 4; Calories 220; Calories from Fat 0; Total Fat 0; Saturated Fat 0; Cholesterol 0; Vitamin A 3% DV; Vitamin C 12% DV; Sodium 3mg (0% DV); Total Carbohydrate 57g (19% DV); Dietary Fiber 2g (8% DV); Protein 1g; Calcium 27% DV; Iron 12%

Microwave Rhubarb Treat

A yummy treat that you can enjoy anytime of year.

4 SERVINGS

Nonstick vegetable cooking spray

3 cups rhubarb, cut into
   1/2-inch pieces

1/3 cup brown sugar

1 tablespoon cornstarch

2/3 cup water

1 teaspoon lemon juice

Topping

1/3 cup flour

1/4 cup brown sugar

1/2 teaspoon cinnamon

2 tablespoons margarine

Spray an 8-inch x 1 1/2-inch round glass baking dish with cooking spray and place rhubarb in it. Thaw (if frozen) in microwave 2 minutes on full power; set aside. In a 2-cup glass container, mix brown sugar with cornstarch. Add water; stir. Microwave, uncovered, 2 to 3 minutes on high power, stirring after each minute, until sauce is thick and bubbling. Add lemon juice. Pour sauce over rhubarb and mix lightly.

In a small bowl, mix flour, brown sugar, and cinnamon for topping. Cut in margarine until crumbly. Sprinkle over rhubarb mixture. Microwave uncovered on high power about 10 minutes, turning dish once, until rhubarb is tender. Serve warm.

(For a conventional oven, bake at 375° for 35 to 40 minutes, or until crumbs are well browned.)

Nutrition Facts (per serving)

Serving size 1/2 cup (235g); Servings per recipe 4; Calories 185; Calories from Fat 54; Total Fat 6g (9% DV); Saturated Fat 1g (5% DV); Cholesterol 0; Vitamin A 7% DV; Vitamin C 11% DV; Sodium 80mg (3% DV); Total Carbohydrate 97g (33% DV); Dietary Fiber 3g (12% DV); Protein 2g; Calcium 8% DV; Iron 9% DV

Rhubarb Peekaboo

So simple. So tasty. And low-fat, too!

16 SERVINGS

Nonstick vegetable cooking spray
18-ounce package white cake mix
4 cups diced rhubarb

1 teaspoon grated lemon rind*
1 cup granulated sugar
Powdered sugar for garnish

Preheat oven to 350°. Spray a 9-inch x 13-inch cake pan with cooking spray. Mix cake as directed on package and pour batter into prepared pan. Top with diced rhubarb and grated rind. Sprinkle granulated sugar over top. Bake for 40 to 50 minutes. Cake is done when center is lightly touched with fingertip and springs back. During baking, the rhubarb and sugar go to the bottom to form a sauce, and the cake rises to the top. Sprinkle top of cake with powdered sugar as a garnish. Serve warm.

*TIP: If you don't have lemon rind on hand, substitute 1/2 teaspoon lemon extract.

Nutrition Facts (per serving)

Serving size 1 square (80g); Servings per recipe 16; Calories 190; Calories from Fat 18; Total Fat 2g (3% DV); Saturated Fat 0; Cholesterol 0; Vitamin A 1% DV; Vitamin C 3% DV; Sodium 250mg (10% DV); Total Carbohydrate 41g (14% DV); Dietary Fiber 1g (4% DV); Protein 2g; Calcium 12% DV; Iron 4%

Rhubarb Crunch

*Coming to us from a neighborhood friend, this recipe is so
good you might just eat up the whole batch yourself before
anyone else gets a taste! You have been warned!*

9 SERVINGS

Nonstick vegetable cooking spray

1 cup sugar

2 tablespoons cornstarch

1 cup water

1 teaspoon vanilla flavoring

1/3 cup melted margarine

1 cup all-purpose flour

1 cup brown sugar

1 teaspoon cinnamon

3/4 cup old-fashioned or quick oats

4 cups diced fresh rhubarb

Preheat oven to 350°. Spray a 9-inch square baking pan with cooking spray and
set aside. In a small saucepan, combine sugar, cornstarch, water, and vanilla flavoring. Cook, stirring constantly, over medium heat until thickened and clear.
Remove from heat and set aside. In a large glass mixing bowl, melt margarine in
the microwave oven. Stir in flour, brown sugar, cinnamon, and oats. Mix until
well blended and crumbly. Put half the dry mixture in baking pan; press firmly to
form a crust. Spread diced rhubarb evenly over the crust. Pour thickened cornstarch mixture over all, and top with remaining crumb mixture. Bake for 1 hour
or until crumb topping is browned. Makes 9 servings.

Nutrition Facts (per serving)

Serving size 1/2 cup (90g); Servings per recipe 9; Calories 155; Calories from Fat 63;
Total Fat 7g (11% DV); Saturated Fat 1g (5% DV); Cholesterol 0; Vitamin A 6% DV;
Vitamin C 3% DV; Sodium 90mg (4% DV); Total Carbohydrate 50g (17% DV);
Dietary Fiber 2g (8% DV); Protein 3g; Calcium 11% DV; Iron 9% DV

Rhubarb Fantasy

Quick, easy, upside-down cake. Not as sweet as one might think.

15 SERVINGS

Nonstick vegetable cooking spray

3 cups diced rhubarb

1 1/3 cups miniature marshmallows

1 cup brown sugar, packed

1/2 cup walnuts, chopped

18-ounce package yellow cake mix

1 cup water

1/2 teaspoon butter flavoring

1/2 teaspoon almond extract

1 teaspoon vanilla flavoring

Whipped topping and grated nutmeg

for garnish

Preheat oven to 350°. Spray a 9-inch x 13-inch pan with cooking spray. Spread rhubarb evenly over bottom of pan. Distribute marshmallows, brown sugar, and nuts evenly over rhubarb. Prepare cake mix using 1 cup water, butter flavoring, almond extract, and vanilla. Beat 2 minutes, scraping sides of bowl often. Pour batter over ingredients in pan. Bake for 45 minutes. Allow to cool to room temperature. Invert on a serving platter. Garnish each serving with a dollop of whipped topping and a dash of grated nutmeg.

Nutrition Facts (per serving)

Serving size 1 piece (105g); Servings per recipe 15; Calories 245; Calories from Fat 45; Total Fat 5g (8% DV); Saturated Fat 1g (5% DV); Cholesterol 0; Vitamin A 1% DV; Vitamin C 3% DV; Sodium 275mg (12% DV); Total Carbohydrate 63g (21% DV); Dietary Fiber 1g (4% DV); Protein 3g; Calcium 10% DV; Iron 7% DV

Glorious Rhubarb Meringue Pie

Tangy, creamy, tasty. Everyone will love it!

8 SERVINGS

1 cup yogurt cheese (see page XX)

3 eggs

1 cup sugar

3 tablespoons flour

1/4 teaspoon salt

1/4 teaspoon almond extract

3 cups rhubarb, cut into 1/2-inch pieces

9-inch unbaked deep dish pastry shell, homemade, frozen, or refrigerated

3 egg whites

1/4 teaspoon cream of tartar

3 tablespoons sugar

1/2 teaspoon vanilla extract

Preheat oven to 425°. Mix together yogurt cheese and eggs until well blended. Add sugar, flour, and salt and mix thoroughly. Stir in extract. Combine creamy mixture with rhubarb and pour into pastry shell. Bake for 45 minutes. Filling is done when custard is firm, or a sharp knife inserted one inch from the edge comes out clean.

Meanwhile, in a very clean, deep metal or glass bowl, whip egg whites until frothy. Sprinkle cream of tartar over egg whites, and continue whipping until egg whites are stiff, but not dry. (Peak tops will bend a bit.) Add sugar 1 tablespoon at a time and whip to dissolve sugar. Add vanilla.

Lower oven temperature to 325°. Spread meringue over baked pie, being certain to seal edges. Bake for 10 to 15 minutes or until delicately browned.

Nutrition Facts (per serving)

Serving size 1 wedge (244g); Servings per recipe 8; Calories 320; Calories from Fat 90; Total Fat 10g (15% DV); Saturated Fat 2g (10% DV); Cholesterol 105mg (35% DV); Vitamin A 3% DV; Vitamin C 6% DV; Sodium 300mg (12% DV); Total Carbohydrate 75g (25% DV); Dietary Fiber 2g (8% DV); Protein 9g; Calcium 21% DV; Iron 8% DV

Rutabagas

HISTORY

Sometimes known as a Swede or a Swedish turnip, the rutabaga is actually a cross between the common turnip and a variety of kale. Thus the rutabaga is a shirttail member of the cabbage family. Sometimes this vegetable is called a "super turnip" because it is bigger and better than an ordinary turnip.

We probably have the rutabaga today because of a fortunate accident in planting. Sometime during the Middle Ages in Europe, an unknown farmer planted turnips and kale near one another and an accidental hybridization occurred, producing the biggest "turnips" the farmer had ever seen. Eaten by the family and by the livestock, this new vegetable was a great success and soon other farmers were planting the new seeds. This vegetable was not identified and described in written records until the 1600s. Called by the English the "turnip-rooted cabbage," the rutabaga is one of the newest vegetables in our food supply.

Warm temperatures can damage rutabaga crops, so they are a special delight of northern climates. Very popular in all northern European lands, but especially the Scandinavian countries, the rutabaga's name even comes from a Swedish word, rotabagge, meaning round root.

SEASON

Like its cousin the turnip, the rutabaga is a cool-season vegetable. The freshly harvested roots occasionally come into the markets beginning in late April. But the
best fresh rutabagas are available in October and November. Minnesota, Washington, Wisconsin, and Canada are the major producers for the North American
market.

QUALITY AND STORAGE

High quality rutabagas are large, elongated, and yellowish. Some people feel that
smaller rutabagas are sweeter than larger ones. Often the globes are coated with
a thin layer of paraffin to retain moisture. The skin, visible through the wax,
should be unblemished. Avoid those with mold on the surface of the wax. Choose
rutabagas that are firm and solid. If they're spongy, they're no longer good.

Rutabagas are exceptionally fine keepers. They store better than turnips and
many other root crops. Keep the roots in plastic bags in the refrigerator. They will
maintain excellent quality for several weeks. They can also be stored at room temperature, although their shelf life will be only about a week.

NUTRITIONAL QUALITY

Rutabagas share with other members of the cruciferous vegetable family the quality of containing goitrogens. These substances, present in small amounts, can
interfere with utilization of iodine by the thyroid gland. People on an iodine-
deficient diet (extremely rare in the United States today) who eat large amounts
of cruciferous vegetables can exaggerate the iodine deficiency and develop goiter,
an enlarged thyroid gland. Because the cruciferous vegetables also contain valuable nutrients and compounds that may reduce risk for cancer, the best approach
is to be sure that you eat plenty of iodine-containing foods (dairy products, fish,
and seafood) and continue to enjoy rutabagas and other cruciferous vegetables
freely.

The rutabaga is a package of nutritional goodness. One-half cup of cooked,
mashed rutabaga contains only 41 calories, virtually no fat, 5% of the Daily Value
for calcium, 43% of the Daily Value for vitamin C, and just over 9% of the Daily
Value for folate. The following table shows how well the rutabaga stacks up compared to turnips and potatoes. All values are shown for one-half cup of the
cooked vegetable.

NUTRIENT	RUTABAGA	TURNIP	WHITE POTATO
Calories	41	22	112
Protein (g)	1	1	2
Fat (g)	<1	<1	<1
Vitamin C (mg)	26	14	15
Folate (mcg)	19	11	11
Calcium (mg)	50	27	6
Iron (mg)	0.6	0.3	0.4

Spice 'n Nice Cake

*A hearty dessert that would complement a
vegetable beef soup supper on a cold winter night.*

16 SERVINGS

Nonstick vegetable cooking spray

2 cups sugar

1/2 cup shortening

4 cups rutabaga, grated
  (about 1 pound)

1 cup applesauce, unsweetened

1 cup water

2 cups all-purpose flour

2 teaspoons baking soda

1 teaspoon baking powder

1/8 teaspoon freshly ground pepper

1/2 teaspoon nutmeg

2 teaspoons cinnamon

1 teaspoon cloves

1 1/2 cups whole wheat flour

1/2 cup chopped nuts

1 cup raisins, plumped*

Quick Maple Icing (recipe below)

Preheat oven to 350°. Spray a 9-inch x 13-inch pan with cooking spray and set aside. Cream together sugar and shortening. Fold in rutabaga and applesauce; add water. Sift all-purpose flour, baking soda, baking powder, and spices together and fold into batter; stir in whole wheat flour, nuts, and raisins. Pour batter into prepared pan and bake for 45 minutes. Cool on rack. Frost with Quick Maple Icing .

*TIP: To plump raisins, soak them in 1 cup water for 10 minutes. Drain thoroughly before adding to batter.

Quick Maple Icing

3 tablespoons margarine

2 cups sifted powdered sugar

1 teaspoon maple flavoring

3 tablespoons skim milk

In a medium bowl mix margarine and powdered sugar. Add flavoring and milk and beat until frosting is uniformly smooth and creamy for easy spreading. If more milk is needed add 1 or 2 teaspoons at a time. Spread between layers and then sides and top of cake.

Nutrition Facts (per serving)

Serving size 1 piece (175g); Servings per recipe 16; Calories 385; Calories from Fat 99; Total Fat 11g (17% DV); Saturated Fat 2g (10% DV); Cholesterol 0; Vitamin A 2% DV; Vitamin C 9% DV; Sodium 170g (7% DV); Total Carbohydrate 70g (23% DV); Dietary Fiber 3g (12% DV; Protein 4g; Calcium 3% DV; Iron 9% DV

Baked Tropical Dessert

Tropical flavors teamed with a surprise ingredient
from the land of the northern lights.

12 SERVINGS

Nonstick vegetable cooking spray

3 cups rutabaga, about 1 pound, peeled,
   cut in matchstick pieces

7-ounce can pineapple tidbits, in juice

1/2 cup brown sugar

1 1/2 teaspoons cinnamon

1/4 teaspoon nutmeg

2 medium apples, sliced thinly

1 1/4 cups all-purpose flour, sifted

1/2 teaspoon baking soda

1/2 cup sugar

1/4 teaspoon salt

1/4 cup margarine, softened

1/2 cup pineapple juice (reserved)

1 cup flaked or shredded coconut

3/4 cup chopped pecans

Preheat oven to 350°. Spray 7-inch x 11-inch or 9-inch x 9-inch pan with cooking spray and set aside. Steam rutabaga about 7 minutes. Drain pineapple tidbits, reserving juice. Combine brown sugar and spices in separate small bowl. Arrange rutabaga, pineapple, and apple in layers in prepared pan, sprinkling sugar mixture between layers. In a separate bowl, combine the flour, soda, sugar, and salt. With a pastry blender or fork, cut in margarine until like coarse meal. Sprinkle over layered vegetable and fruits in pan. Pour pineapple juice over all ingredients; sprinkle with coconut and pecans. Bake for 1 hour. Serve warm.

Nutrition Facts (per serving)

Serving size 1/2 cup (135g); Servings per recipe 12; Calories 200; Calories from Fat 45; Total Fat 5g (8% DV); Saturated Fat 0; Cholesterol 0; Vitamin A 1% DV; Vitamin C 15% DV; Sodium 100mg (4% DV); Total Carbohydrate 39g (13% DV); Dietary Fiber 3g (12% DV); Protein 2g; Calcium 3% DV; Iron 7% DV

Squash

HISTORY

Squashes are closely related to pumpkins, cucumbers, and gourds. In fact, some botanists say these are all just types of squash. There are two large branches of the squash family—summer squash and winter squash. Summer squashes ripen quickly during the summer. They have deep or pale green or yellow skins with a pale, watery flesh. Their mild, neutral flavor favors their use in nearly every dessert from cupcakes to soufflés.

Winter squash matures after a long season and has a tough rind and a large central seed cavity. Looking like Arabian turbans or overweight gourds, winter squashes have deep orange flesh and a mildly sweet taste, perfect for nourishing desserts.

Squash is a vegetable gift from the New World to the Old. Native Americans considered summer squash, although edible, to be a mystic plant of great power. Among the Hopi, the squash blossom is a symbol of fertility. Columbus noted zucchini growing where he visited on his first voyage. Later voyagers found it growing across the entire North and South American continents.

European settlers in North America quickly adopted the squash and made it an important part of their diet. Our English word *squash* comes from the original Native American name for the vegetable. Thomas Jefferson and George Washington, both enthusiastic gardeners, grew squash on their plantations.

Introduced into England around 1700, summer squash quickly became popular and was grown in many a kitchen garden. Summer squash is a big family
with many members, including zucchini, crookneck, straightneck, and pattypan.

Zucchini, the most familiar of summer squashes, is so popular today that
whole cookbooks have been devoted to this one vegetable alone. As every home
gardener knows, zucchini plants produce abundantly. Every summer, zucchini
mysteriously appears in the break rooms of offices, as gardeners share their too-
large harvest. In fact, August 8 each year is listed in a national calendar of events
as National Sneak-Some-Zucchini-Onto-Your-Neighbor's-Porch Night.

Winter squash is of Central American origin. Seeds have been found in archeological digs of 5000 BC in Mexico and 3000 BC in Peru. Again, there is a confusion of names because there are many winter squashes: hubbard, turban, acorn,
buttercup, butternut, spaghetti, and banana. While some squashes are named for
their shape, spaghetti squash is unique in being named for its string-like interior,
a dead ringer for a tangle of cooked spaghetti pasta.

Native Americans sliced the ripe winter squash thinly and dried it for use during the bleak winter months. Europeans adapted the summer squash to folk medicinal purposes, binding the rind to the forehead to cure running eyes and using
the flesh as a cosmetic. The seeds were rubbed on freckles and spots to make them
disappear.

SEASON

Although summer squashes are most plentiful from May through September, you
may be able to find fresh summer squash (at least zucchini) year-round in your
supermarket. In contrast, winter squashes are at their peak beginning in late summer and continuing through the fall and winter. By spring, it will be difficult to
find fresh winter squash. Acorn squash tends to be more available and may be
found all year. Cooked winter squash is available all year in frozen form.

QUALITY AND STORAGE

Summer squash is most delicious when immature. If allowed to become too
large, it loses much quality. The flesh becomes stringy and the seeds grow large
and tough. Choose summer squashes that are small, firm, and heavy for their size.
Flabby squashes have lost water and quality. Heaviness indicates good water content. Lightweight summer squashes are likely to be dry and woody. Since the rind

is thin, it is easily damaged. Look for squash with intact skin that is glossy and evenly colored.

Summer squash does not have a long storage life. Store it in a plastic bag in the crisper drawer of the refrigerator to maintain moisture. It should store well for 1 to 2 weeks.

Winter squash is best when allowed to mature. The longer the squash grows (and the bigger it becomes), the sweeter it will be. If you can use the queen size squash, then by all means buy it. If it will go to waste, then choose a smaller one. Beyond size, look for a smooth, dry, unblemished rind. Cracks or spots will be points for early rot and decay. The skin should be dull. A shiny skin is a sign the squash was picked before reaching maturity and will not be as sweet. Lift the winter squash and feel its weight. It should feel heavy for its size. If you are buying a cut, plastic-wrapped piece (some of those squashes are just too big!), look for deep orange color and fine-grained flesh.

One of the champion storers, winter squash will keep in a cool, dry place like the basement for 3 months or perhaps even longer. Do not store in the refrigerator. This is one vegetable that deteriorates in the refrigerator. However, once the squash has been cut open, it must be kept refrigerated. Cut squash will keep about a week if tightly covered in plastic wrap.

NUTRITIONAL QUALITY

Summer squash is more than 95% water, so it is low in calories. One cup of raw summer squash has a meager 26 calories—a good weight-loss food! In that cup you also get 1/3 of the Daily Value for vitamin C, 5% of the Daily Value for vitamin A, and 16% of the Daily Value for folate. Mineral content is fairly low. Because of the watery nature of summer squash, dietary fiber content is modest—7% of the Daily Value in 1 cup of raw squash.

Winter squash is a superstar in the vegetable world. Its deep orange flesh reveals the secret—a rich vein of better-than-gold beta-carotene. For only 83 calories, one cup of cooked butternut squash will give you 1/2 your Daily Value for vitamin C and 287% of your Daily Value for vitamin A. As if you could expect a food to give you anything more, as a bonus, that same cup of cooked winter squash provides 8% of the Daily Value for calcium, 7% of the Daily Value for iron, and 27% of the Daily Value for dietary fiber.

Both dietary fiber and beta-carotene have been identified by recent research as important food components that help prevent cancer. Beta-carotene, the plant form of vitamin A, is also essential for healthy skin and membranes, good vision, and a healthy immune system. Bring on the squash!

Zucchini Brownies

Yummy!

24 SERVINGS

Nonstick vegetable cooking spray

1 cup all-purpose flour

1 teaspoon cinnamon

1 teaspoon baking soda

3 tablespoons unsweetened cocoa

1/2 teaspoon salt

1 cup whole wheat flour

1 1/2 cups sugar

1/2 cup vegetable oil

1 egg

2 1/2 cups grated, unpeeled zucchini

1 cup mini chocolate chips

2 tablespoons sugar

1/2 cup wheat germ

Preheat oven to 350°. Spray a 9-inch x 13-inch pan with cooking spray. Stir together all-purpose flour, cinnamon, baking soda, cocoa, and salt. Stir in wheat flour; set aside. Beat together sugar, oil, and egg. Fold in dry ingredients. Stir in zucchini. Pour batter into prepared pan. Mix last 3 ingredients together and sprinkle over batter. Bake for 30 minutes, or until brownies pull away slightly from edge of pan. Cut into 24 pieces (4 by 6).

Nutrition Facts (per serving)

Serving size 1 brownie (60g); Servings per recipe 24; Calories 185; Calories from Fat 72; Total Fat 8g (12% DV); Saturated Fat 2g (10% DV); Cholesterol 11mg (4% DV; Vitamin A 4% DV; Vitamin C 5% DV; Sodium 115mg (5% DV); Total Carbohydrate 29g (10% DV); Dietary Fiber 2g (8% DV); Protein 3g; Calcium 1% DV; Iron 8% DV

Spicy Zucchini Bars

Quick and delicious.

24 SERVINGS

Nonstick vegetable cooking spray	*3 egg whites*
2 cups all-purpose flour	*1/2 cup vegetable oil*
1 teaspoon baking powder	*1/2 cup brown sugar, packed*
1 teaspoon baking soda	*1 cup plain fat-free yogurt*
2 teaspoons cinnamon	*1 teaspoon vanilla flavoring*
1/4 teaspoon ground cloves	*1 1/2 cups shredded, unpeeled zucchini*
1/4 teaspoon salt	*2 tablespoons powdered sugar*

Preheat oven to 350°. Spray a 9-inch x 13-inch baking pan with cooking spray and set aside. Combine flour, baking powder, baking soda, cinnamon, cloves, and salt and set aside. Combine egg whites, oil, brown sugar, yogurt, and vanilla flavoring in a large bowl; beat well. Stir in zucchini; add flour mixture and stir until well blended. Pour batter into prepared pan. Bake for 30 minutes. To test for doneness bars should spring back when touched lightly with finger. Cool in pan. Sprinkle with powdered sugar and cut into 24 bars (4 by 6).

Nutrition Facts (per serving)

Serving size 1 bar (45g); Servings per recipe 24; Calories 105; Calories from Fat 45; Total Fat 5g (8% DV); Saturated Fat 1g (5% DV); Cholesterol 0 (0% DV); Vitamin A 1% DV; Vitamin C 1% DV; Sodium 85mg (4% DV); Total Carbohydrate 14g (5% DV); Dietary Fiber 1g (4% DV); Protein 2g; Calcium 3% DV; Iron 4% DV

Cocoa Zucchini Cake

*A **big** cake that is big on flavor and nutrition!*

16 SERVINGS

Nonstick vegetable cooking spray

1 1/2 cups all-purpose flour

1 cup whole wheat flour

1 cup wheat germ

1/2 cup unsweetened cocoa

2 1/2 teaspoons baking powder

1 1/2 teaspoons baking soda

1 teaspoon salt

1 teaspoon cinnamon

3/4 cup vegetable oil

2 cups sugar

3 egg whites

2 teaspoons vanilla flavoring

2 teaspoons orange extract

2 cups grated, unpeeled zucchini

3/4 cup skim milk

Vanilla Glaze (recipe below)

Preheat oven to 350°. Spray a 10-inch tube pan with cooking spray; dust with flour, then set aside. Combine all-purpose flour, whole wheat flour, wheat germ, cocoa, baking powder, baking soda, salt, and cinnamon and set aside. With an electric mixer, beat oil and sugar until blended. Add egg whites. Stir in vanilla flavoring, orange extract, and zucchini. Alternately stir in dry ingredients and milk. Pour batter into prepared pan. Bake for 1 hour or until toothpick inserted in center comes out clean. Cool in pan 15 minutes; turn onto wire rack to cool. Drizzle glaze over cake.

Vanilla Glaze

2 cups powdered sugar

3 tablespoons skim milk

1 teaspoon vanilla extract

Combine ingredients and beat until smooth. Drizzle over cake.

Nutrition Facts (per serving)

Serving size 1 slice (140g); Servings per recipe 16; Calories 430; Calories from Fat 99; Total Fat 11g (17% DV); Saturated Fat 2g (10% DV); Cholesterol 0; Vitamin A 10% V; Vitamin C 11% DV; Sodium 365mg (15% DV); Total Carbohydrate 81g (27% DV); Dietary Fiber 3g (12% DV); Protein 6g; Calcium 5% DV; Iron 15% DV

Butterscotch Cookies

A sweet finale to a trip to the local farmers' market.

6 DOZEN

*Nonstick vegetable cooking
spray*

1/4 cup honey

1 1/2 cups brown sugar, packed

3/4 cup margarine, softened

1 egg

1 teaspoon vanilla flavoring

Grated rind of 1 orange

*3 cups grated, unpeeled crookneck
squash*

1/2 cups all-purpose flour

1 teaspoon baking soda

1 teaspoon salt

3 cups quick-cooking oats

1/2 cup wheat germ

1 cup butterscotch chips

Preheat oven to 375°. Lightly spray cookie sheets with cooking spray; set aside. Cream honey, brown sugar, and margarine. Beat egg into mixture; add vanilla and orange rind. Fold in squash. Sift flour, baking soda, and salt into squash mixture. Stir until flour is completely mixed into batter. Fold in oats, wheat germ, and butterscotch chips. Dough will be sticky. Drop by spoonfuls onto prepared cookie sheet. Bake for 12 to 15 minutes or until cookies are slightly browned. Remove cookies from baking sheet to cooling rack. Cool thoroughly before storing.

Nutrition Facts (per serving)

Serving size 1 cookie (25g); Servings per recipe 72; Calories 75; Calories from Fat 27; Total Fat 3g (5% DV); Saturated Fat 1g (5% DV); Cholesterol 4mg (1% DV); Vitamin A 3% DV; Vitamin C 2% DV; Sodium 75mg (3% DV); Total Carbohydrate 11g (4% DV); Dietary Fiber 1g (4% DV); Protein 1g; Calcium 1% DV; Iron 3% DV

Golden Lemon Cake

Everything is golden with this dessert.

16 SERVINGS

Nonstick vegetable cooking spray

18-ounce package lemon cake mix

1/3 cup vegetable oil

2 eggs

2 cups grated, unpeeled summer squash

3/4 cup unsweetened crushed

pineapple, well drained

1/2 cup sliced almonds

Preheat oven to 325°. Spray a 9-inch x 13-inch pan° with cooking spray and set aside. In a large mixing bowl, beat together the cake mix, oil, and eggs at low speed until moistened. Continue beating at medium speed for 2 minutes. Fold in squash, pineapple, and almonds, thoroughly blending all ingredients. Pour batter into prepared pan and bake for 45 to 55 minutes. Cake is done when a toothpick inserted in center comes out clean. A cream cheese frosting would be a good accompaniment if you prefer frosted cakes.

°TIP: A 12-cup Bundt pan can also be used. Bake for 60 to 70 minutes.

Nutrition Facts (per serving)

Serving size 1 piece (80g); Servings per recipe 16; Calories 215; Calories from Fat 90; Total Fat 10g (15% DV); Saturated Fat 2g (10% DV); Cholesterol 34mg (11% DV); Vitamin A 2% DV; Vitamin C 4% DV; Sodium 220mg (9% DV); Total Carbohydrate 31g (10% DV); Dietary Fiber 2g (8% DV); Protein 3g; Calcium 8% DV; Iron 5% DV

Summer Sunshine Cake

The first squash of the season brings a moist cake to the table.
At the end of summer, use zucchini squash for an equally moist taste treat.

12 SERVINGS

Nonstick vegetable cooking spray

1 cup all-purpose flour

1 cup whole wheat flour

2 teaspoons baking soda

1 teaspoon cinnamon

1 teaspoon nutmeg

1/4 teaspoon salt

1/2 cup margarine, softened

2 cups sugar

2 eggs

1 tablespoon grated orange peel

1/3 cup orange juice

2 cups grated, unpeeled summer
squash

Low-fat whipped topping or
Nutmeg Rum Sauce (recipe below)

Preheat oven to 400°. Spray a 9-inch x 13-inch cake pan with cooking spray; set aside. Stir together flours, baking soda, cinnamon, nutmeg, and salt. In large bowl, cream margarine with sugar and eggs until light and fluffy. Fold in half of flour mixture. Stir grated rind and orange juice into batter, and add remaining flour mixture. Fold in squash and pour batter into prepared pan. Bake for 40 to 45 minutes or until cake tester inserted in center comes out clean. Be careful not to overbake or cake will be tough. Cut warm cake into 12 squares and serve with low-fat whipped topping or Nutmeg Rum Sauce.

Nutmeg Rum Sauce

2 tablespoons cornstarch

1 cup sugar

1 cup water

1/4 teaspoon ground nutmeg

2 to 3 tablespoons rum, or 1/2 to
1 tablespoon rum flavoring

2 teaspoons margarine

Mix cornstarch and sugar in heavy saucepan. Add water, bring to a boil, and cook, stirring constantly, until clear and thickened. Remove from heat and stir in nutmeg, rum or rum flavoring, and margarine. Serve warm over cake.

Nutrition Facts (per serving)

Serving size 1 square with 3 tablespoons sauce (165g); Servings per recipe 12; Calories 365; Calories from Fat 90; Total Fat 10g (15% DV); Saturated Fat 2g (10% DV); Cholesterol 46mg (15% DV); Vitamin A 9% DV; Vitamin C 7% DV; Sodium 290mg (12% DV); Total Carbohydrate 68g (23% DV); Dietary Fiber 2g (8% DV); Protein 4g; Calcium 3% DV; Iron 7% DV

Soft Spaghetti Cookies

Take them to the next potluck and watch them disappear.

48 COOKIES

Nonstick vegetable cooking spray

2 cups spaghetti squash

2 1/2 cups all-purpose flour

1 teaspoon baking powder

1 1/2 teaspoons baking soda

1 teaspoon salt

1 teaspoon cinnamon

1 teaspoon nutmeg

1/2 teaspoon cloves

3/4 cup shortening

1/2 cup sugar

1 cup brown sugar

2 eggs

2 teaspoons vanilla flavoring

1/2 cup wheat germ

3/4 cup raisins

1/2 cup chopped nuts

Creamy Orange Frosting

(recipe below)

Preheat oven to 375°. Spray cookie sheets with cooking spray; set aside. Cut squash in half and remove seeds. Scoop out squash flesh to measure 2 cups and set aside. Sift together dry ingredients. Cream shortening and sugars. Beat in eggs and vanilla; stir in wheat germ. Add dry ingredients alternately with spaghetti squash. Stir in raisins and nuts. Drop by teaspoonfuls onto baking sheet. Bake for 10 to 12 minutes until edges begin to brown. When cool, frost with Creamy Orange Frosting.

Creamy Orange Frosting

1/2 tub (4-ounces) light cream cheese, softened

2 cups powdered sugar, sifted

2 tablespoons orange juice

1 1/2 teaspoons grated orange rind

Blend cream cheese and sugar until thoroughly mixed. Stir in orange juice and orange rind.

Nutrition Facts (per serving)

Serving size 1 cookie (35g); Servings per recipe 48; Calories 120; Calories from Fat 45; Total Fat 5g (8% DV); Saturated Fat 1g (5% DV); Cholesterol 13mg (4% DV); Vitamin A 2% DV; Vitamin C 3% DV; Sodium 85mg (3% DV); Total Carbohydrate 19g (6% DV); Dietary Fiber 2g (8% DV); Protein 2g; Calcium 1% DV; Iron 4% DV

Spaghetti and Cider Cake

Apple cider and honey whisper cozy comfort.

24 SERVINGS

Nonstick vegetable cooking spray

1 1/2 cups spaghetti squash, firmly packed

1/2 cup apple cider

1/2 cup honey

1 cup dark brown sugar

1/2 cup applesauce

1/2 cup buttermilk*

3 eggs, beaten

3 cups all-purpose flour

1 teaspoon salt

1 teaspoon baking soda

2 1/2 teaspoons baking powder

1 teaspoon cinnamon

1/2 teaspoon nutmeg

1/2 teaspoon allspice

1/2 cup sunflower kernels

Preheat oven to 350°. Spray a 9-inch x 13-inch pan with cooking spray; set aside. Cut spaghetti squash in half and remove seeds. Scoop out 1 1/2 cups of flesh and simmer it in cider until tender. In a large bowl, cream honey, brown sugar, and applesauce. Gradually add buttermilk and eggs. Beat well. Mix dry ingredients together and add to squash mixture. Fold in sunflower kernels. Pour into prepared pan. Bake for 50 to 55 minutes. Cake is done when toothpick inserted in center comes out clean. Cut into 24 pieces (4 by 6).

*TIP: Reconstituted powdered buttermilk can be used.

Nutrition Facts (per serving)

Serving size 1 square (70g); Servings per recipe 24; Calories 160; Calories from Fat 27; Total Fat 3g (5% DV); Saturated Fat 0; Cholesterol 34mg (11% DV); Vitamin A 1% DV; Vitamin C 1% DV; Sodium 175mg (7% DV); Total Carbohydrate 30g (10% DV); Dietary Fiber 1g (4% DV); Protein 4g; Calcium 4% DV; Iron 8% DV

Orange Spaghetti Cake

A moist, practically fat-free cake.

16 SERVINGS

Nonstick vegetable cooking spray	1 cup sugar
2 cups spaghetti squash	1/2 cup applesauce
4 cups all-purpose flour	1/2 cup skim milk
1 tablespoon baking powder	1 1/2 tablespoons grated orange rind
1 teaspoon salt	2/3 cup orange juice
1/4 teaspoon baking soda	1/2 cup golden raisins
3 eggs, beaten	Creamy Orange Frosting (recipe below)

Preheat oven to 350°. Spray a Bundt pan with cooking spray, lightly flour it, and set aside. Cut spaghetti squash in half and remove seeds. Scoop out 2 cups of flesh. Sift together flour, baking powder, salt, and baking soda. In large bowl beat eggs; add sugar, applesauce, and squash. Stir in milk, orange rind, and orange juice. Fold flour mixture into batter. Fold in golden raisins. Pour batter into prepared pan and bake for about 30 minutes or until toothpick inserted in center comes out clean. When cool, frost with Creamy Orange Frosting.

Creamy Orange Frosting

1/2 tub (4 ounces) light cream cheese	2 tablespoons orange juice
2 cups powdered sugar, sifted	1 1/2 teaspoons grated orange rind

Blend cream cheese and powdered sugar until smooth. Stir in orange juice and orange rind.

Nutrition Facts (per serving)

Serving size 1 piece (125g); Servings per recipe 16; Calories 265; Calories from Fat 27; Total Fat 3g (5% DV); Saturated Fat 1g (5% DV); Cholesterol 55mg (18% DV); Vitamin A 4% DV; Vitamin C 11% DV; Sodium 235mg (10% DV); Total Carbohydrate 56g (19% DV); Dietary Fiber 2g (8% DV); Protein 5g; Calcium 4% DV; Iron 10% DV

Autumn Gold

*This colorful frozen dessert will get your family
eating winter squash and asking for more.*

12 SERVINGS

2 12-ounce packages frozen winter squash, thawed	1/4 teaspoon cloves
1 cup sugar	1 teaspoon cinnamon
1/4 teaspoon salt	1 pint hazelnut flavor non-dairy creamer
1/4 teaspoon ginger	18 gingersnaps

Cook squash in microwave on high power for 4 minutes; stir. Cook another 4 minutes; stir. Add sugar, salt, and spices; cook another 3 minutes. Chill.

After mixture is cool, stir in creamer. Freeze according to directions in an ice-cream maker. Or pour into a shallow pan and place in freezer. Stir every 30 minutes for about 2 hours until the mixture is soft frozen.

Crush gingersnaps in food processor or blender or by placing gingersnaps in a plastic bag and crushing with a rolling pin. Put a very thin layer of crumbs in bottom of a 9-inch springform pan; spoon in half the frozen mixture. Add a layer of about 3/4 of the crumbs; spoon in remaining frozen mixture and top with remaining crumbs. Cover with foil or plastic wrap and freeze several hours or overnight.

Let stand at room temperature 10 minutes before serving.

Nutrition Facts (per serving)

Serving size 1/2 cup (125g); Servings per recipe 12; Calories 170; Calories from Fat 36; Total Fat 4g (6% DV); Saturated Fat 4g (20% DV); Cholesterol 4mg (1% DV); Vitamin A 43% DV; Vitamin C 10% DV; Sodium 145mg (6% DV); Total Carbohydrate 32g (11% DV); Dietary Fiber 3g (12% DV); Protein 1g; Calcium 2% DV; Iron 2% DV

Harvest Time Doughnuts

Serve them hot and start a Halloween tradition.

36 SERVINGS

Oil for deep-fat frying

1 cup sugar

1 tablespoon shortening

2 eggs, beaten

1 1/2 cups cooked, mashed winter squash

1 teaspoon vanilla flavoring

4 1/2 cups all-purpose flour

3 teaspoons baking powder

1/2 teaspoon salt

1/2 teaspoon nutmeg

1/2 teaspoon cinnamon

1 cup skim milk

Cream together sugar and shortening. Stir in eggs, squash, and vanilla. Fold in flour, baking powder, and spices alternately with the milk, ending with flour. Cover and chill dough for at least an hour.

Heat oil to 375°. Correct temperature is vital to avoid excessive fat absorption. On a floured board, pat (or roll) dough 1/2-inch thick and cut with doughnut cutter. The dough should be soft yet firm enough that it doesn't stick to board. Allow to sit after cutting for 10 to 12 minutes so doughnuts will absorb less fat. Drop doughnuts one or two at a time into the hot oil. Turn doughnuts as they brown so both sides cook. Drain on paper towels. Dust with powdered sugar or granulated sugar or serve them plain—but do serve them while still warm!

Nutrition Facts (per serving)

Serving size 1 doughnut (45g); Servings per recipe 36; Calories 125; Calories from Fat 45; Total Fat 5g (8% DV); Saturated Fat 1g (5% DV); Cholesterol 15mg (5% DV); Vitamin A 7% DV; Vitamin C 2% DV; Sodium 65mg (3% DV); Total Carbohydrate 19g (6% DV); Dietary Fiber 1g (4% DV); Protein 2g; Calcium 2% DV; Iron 4% DV

Chill Out Squash Pie

Mellow flavor with a remarkable crust.

8 SERVINGS

1/4 cup brown sugar

10-ounce package frozen squash, thawed

1/2 teaspoon cinnamon

1/4 teaspoon ginger

Dash nutmeg

1/4 teaspoon salt

1 quart low-fat vanilla ice cream

Oatmeal Crust (see page 103)

1/3 cup broken pecans

Combine brown sugar, squash, spices, and salt in a medium saucepan. Stirring constantly, bring just to a boil. Remove from heat. Set aside to cool.

Stir softened ice cream to be certain it is all the same consistency. Fold cooled squash mixture into ice cream; set in freezer for 12 to 15 minutes. Remove filling from freezer when outer edge is quite firm. Stir until mixture is the same consistency and return to the freezer for about 15 minutes; remove, stir, and then pour into cooled oatmeal crust. Cover with plastic wrap and freeze until firm. This procedure will prevent ice crystals from forming and give a smoother texture. Garnish with pecan pieces and, if desired, a dollop of low-fat whipped topping and a sprinkle of ground cloves.

Nutrition Facts (per serving)

Serving size 1 wedge (135g); Servings per recipe 8; Calories 275; Calories from Fat 108; Total Fat 12g (18% DV); Saturated Fat 3g (15% DV); Cholesterol 9mg (3% DV); Vitamin A 30% DV; Vitamin C 6% DV; Sodium 190mg (8% DV); Total Carbohydrate 38g (13% DV); Dietary Fiber 2g (8% DV); Protein 5g; Calcium 11% DV; Iron 6% DV

Nutty Winter Squash Pie

*Even if you think you don't like squash, you'll
ask for a second piece of this wonderful baked pie.*

10 SERVINGS

2 cups pureed, cooked winter squash	1/4 teaspoon nutmeg
1 cup sugar	3 eggs
1/2 teaspoon salt	12-ounce can evaporated skim milk
1 teaspoon cinnamon	2 tablespoons chopped pecans
1/2 teaspoon ginger	10-inch unbaked pastry shell,
1/4 teaspoon ground cloves	homemade or refrigerated

Preheat oven to 425°. Combine squash, sugar, and seasonings in a bowl and mix well; add eggs and beat well. Stir in milk. Pour mixture into pie shell and sprinkle pecans over top. Bake for 15 minutes, then reduce oven temperature to 350° for 45 minutes, or until a knife inserted halfway between center and edge comes out clean. Cool on rack. If desired, serve with a dollop of low-fat whipped topping.

Nutrition Facts (per serving)

Serving size 1 wedge (135g); Servings per recipe 10; Calories 245; Calories from Fat 81; Total Fat 9g (14% DV); Saturated Fat 2g (10% DV); Cholesterol 85mg (28% DV); Vitamin A 34% DV; Vitamin C 8% DV; Sodium 280mg (12% DV); Total Carbohydrate 37g (12% DV); Dietary Fiber 2g (8% DV); Protein 6g; Calcium 13% DV; Iron 6% DV

Black Walnut Cake

Everyone will delight in the flavor!

16 SERVINGS

Nonstick vegetable cooking spray

1/2 cup applesauce

2 eggs, beaten

1 cup cooked, mashed squash

1 cup brown sugar, packed

3 cups cake flour, sifted

4 teaspoons baking powder

1/4 teaspoon baking soda

1/2 teaspoon salt

1 cup skim milk

1 teaspoon maple flavoring

1 cup chopped black walnuts *

Quick Maple Icing (recipe below)

Preheat oven to 350°. Spray a 9-inch x 13-inch or two 9-inch layer cake pans with cooking spray; set aside. In a large bowl, combine applesauce, eggs, squash, and brown sugar. Beat until thoroughly mixed. Sift together dry ingredients; add to batter with milk and maple flavoring. Fold in black walnuts. Pour batter into prepared pan and bake for 30 minutes, or until toothpick inserted in center comes out clean. Frost with Quick Maple Icing.

*TIP: If black walnuts are not available, substitute English walnuts and add 1 1/2 teaspoons black walnut extract as well as the maple flavoring.

Quick Maple Icing

3 tablespoons margarine

2 cups sifted powdered sugar

1 teaspoon maple flavoring

3 tablespoons skim milk

In a medium bowl, mix margarine and powdered sugar. Add flavoring and milk and beat until frosting is uniformly smooth and creamy for easy spreading. If more milk is needed add 1 or 2 teaspoons at a time. Spread between layers and then sides and top of cake.

Nutrition Facts (per serving)

Serving size 1 piece (100g); Servings per recipe 16; Calories 255; Calories from Fat 72; Total Fat 8g (12% DV); Saturated Fat 1g (5% DV); Cholesterol 35mg (12% DV); Vitamin A 13% DV; Vitamin C 2% DV; Sodium 210mg (9% DV); Total Carbohydrate 44g (15% DV); Dietary Fiber 1g (4% DV); Protein 5g; Calcium 6% DV; Iron 8% DV

Easy Spice Cake

A moist cake that is high in nutrition, yet even higher in flavor.

12 SERVINGS

Nonstick vegetable cooking spray

18-ounce package spice cake mix

1 cup pureed winter squash

1/2 cup skim milk

1/3 cup vegetable oil

2 eggs

Preheat oven to 350°. Spray a 9-inch x 13-inch pan or a 12-cup Bundt pan and with cooking spray, and set aside. In a large mixing bowl beat cake mix, squash, milk, vegetable oil, and eggs at low speed until moistened. Then beat at medium speed for 2 minutes. Pour into prepared pan and bake for 35 to 40 minutes for 9-inch x 13-inch pan or 40 to 45 minutes for Bundt pan. Cool for 10 minutes in pan. Remove from pan if you choose and cool completely on wire rack.

Nutrition Facts (per serving)

Serving size 1 piece (85g); Servings per recipe 12; Calories 255; Calories from Fat 99; Total Fat 11g (17% DV); Saturated Fat 3g (15% DV); Cholesterol 45mg (15% DV); Vitamin A 13% DV; Vitamin C 3% DV; Sodium 315mg (13% DV); Total Carbohydrate 36g (12% DV); Dietary Fiber 1g (4% DV); Protein 4g; Calcium 12% DV; Iron 5% DV

Notabanana Cookies

Kids will love the name and the taste.

6 DOZEN

3/4 cup margarine, softened	1/2 teaspoon cinnamon
1 1/2 cups sugar	1/2 teaspoon cloves
2 eggs, beaten	1/2 teaspoon ginger
2 teaspoons vanilla flavoring	1/2 teaspoon allspice
3 cups all-purpose flour	3 cups grated, raw banana squash
1/2 teaspoon salt	1 cup wheat germ
2 tablespoons baking powder	1 cup golden raisins
1 1/4 teaspoons baking soda	1/2 cup chopped nuts

Preheat oven to 350°. Blend margarine and sugar. Add eggs and vanilla. Sift together flour, salt, baking powder, baking soda, and spices. Gradually blend dry ingredients into egg mixture. Fold in banana squash, wheat germ, raisins, and nuts. Drop by teaspoonfuls onto ungreased baking sheet. Bake for 10 to 12 minutes, or until lightly browned.

Nutrition Facts (per serving)

Serving size 1 cookie (26g); Servings per recipe 72; Calories 75; Calories from Fat 27; Total Fat 3g (5% DV); Saturated Fat 0; Cholesterol 8mg (3% DV); Vitamin A 4% DV; Vitamin C 3% DV; Sodium 100mg (4% DV); Total Carbohydrate 12g (4% DV); Dietary Fiber 1g (4% DV); Protein 1g; Calcium 1% DV; Iron 4%

Squash-Date Loaf

Think of it as a veggie pound cake and you will love it.

16 SERVINGS

Nonstick vegetable cooking spray	1/2 teaspoon salt
1 cup pureed, cooked banana squash	1/2 teaspoon baking powder
1/3 cup skim milk	1/2 teaspoon cinnamon
1 teaspoon vanilla flavoring	1/2 teaspoon allspice
1 cup all-purpose flour	1/2 cup chopped dates
3/4 cup sugar	1/2 cup chopped nuts

Preheat oven to 350°. Spray a 9-inch x 5-inch loaf pan with cooking spray and set aside. Cut banana squash in half, and scoop out seeds. Cut squash half into large chunks; place cut-side up in a shallow microwavable dish. Cover and cook until tender, rotating the dish halfway through the cooking time. Total cooking time will be about 7 to 8 minutes. Scoop flesh from rind, then puree in blender or food processor or mash by hand. Pack into cup to measure.

Combine squash, milk, and vanilla in large mixing bowl. Sift together dry ingredients and add to squash mixture. Fold in dates and nuts. Pour batter into prepared pan. Bake for 60 to 75 minutes, or until toothpick inserted in center comes out clean.

Nutrition Facts (per serving)

Serving size 1 slice (45g); Servings per recipe 16; Calories 110; Calories from Fat 18; Total Fat 2g (3% DV); Saturated Fat 0; Cholesterol 0; Vitamin A 1% DV; Vitamin C 1% DV; Sodium 80mg (3% DV); Total Carbohydrate 21g (7% DV); Dietary Fiber 1g (4% DV); Protein 2g; Calcium 2% DV; Iron 3% DV

Sweet Potatoes

HISTORY

The sweet potato has been called by 151 different names in various documents. The most common synonym for this root vegetable is yam. But these are really two different vegetables altogether, and the plants do not look at all alike.

Some people erroneously distinguish between sweet potatoes and yams on the basis of moisture. They claim the yam is moister and the sweet potato drier. In fact, there is a wide range of moisture content in sweet potatoes, so this distinction is not always accurate.

Only sweet potatoes are grown within the United States. When true yams appear in the market, they have been imported. The U.S. Department of Agriculture requires that all sweet potatoes grown in the United States be labeled as "sweet potatoes," not as "yams." In practice, Americans use the two terms interchangeably, and the two vegetables can be used interchangeably in recipes as well.

The sweet potato is native to the Western Hemisphere. Used as food since prehistoric times in tropical America and on South Pacific islands, this sweet vegetable was carried to the rest of the world by the Europeans who explored the New World. Columbus saw the natives eating sweet potatoes in the West Indies and returned to Europe with the new food. The native American name for the vegetable was batata or padada. Spaniards adopted the native name and hence, today, the sweet "potato."

If you want to eat a food with glamour, the sweet potato has it. In an interview in *People* magazine, Cher revealed that she and Michelle Pfieffer both enjoy the sweet potato frequently because it is an easy microwavable snack.

SEASON

Fresh sweet potatoes are available all year. Like other root crops they are in the market without regard to season.

QUALITY AND STORAGE

Select firm roots without bruises or soft spots. The darker orange the sweet potatoes, the higher the nutritional quality will be. Handle them carefully to prevent bruising. Store fresh sweet potatoes in a dry, unrefrigerated place at 55 to 60 degrees. Do not refrigerate this tropical vegetable. Cold temperatures chill it, making the core hard, and imparting an undesirable taste.

Sweet potatoes become sweeter if they are "cured" after being freshly dug. Sweet potatoes purchased in the supermarket have been out of the ground for several days and are already cured. Sweet potatoes fresh from the garden will taste better and cook more easily if they are stored a few days before use.

Sweet potatoes can be frozen after cooking. Wash and bake or boil in the skin until slightly soft. If boiled, drain and pat dry. Wrap each sweet potato, skin on, individually in plastic wrap and place in freezer bags.

Canned or frozen sweet potatoes can be substituted for fresh sweet potatoes in any recipe calling for the cooked vegetable as an ingredient. Canned sweet potatoes are generally smaller than the fresh ones in the market. Six to eight canned sweet potatoes equal approximately four medium-sized fresh ones.

NUTRITIONAL QUALITY

The sweet potato is a superstar vegetable. One medium sweet potato provides 200% of the Daily Value for vitamin A at a cost of only 141 calories. Beta-carotene, the plant form of vitamin A, is deep orange in color. Pale orange or yellow sweet potatoes contain less beta-carotene than dark orange sweet potatoes.

In addition, the sweet potato has 42% of the Daily Value for vitamin C and 10% of the Daily Value for iron. Sweet potatoes are low in sodium, high in potassium, virtually fat free, and high in dietary fiber. The sweet potato fits all of today's dietary recommendations.

Another value of the sweet potato is that several strains are naturally resistant to pests. This means that no chemical pesticides are used in their cultivation.

Vitamin A, the nutrient treasure locked within the sweet potato, performs many functions essential for good health. It's vital for vision in the dark. Vitamin A is actually part of the pigment in the eye that allows you to see. Vitamin A helps keep membranes and skin healthy and strengthens your ability to fight infection. Recent research has found yet another role for vitamin A. It detoxifies certain environmental pollutants to which we are exposed.

Several scientists who conduct research on diet and cancer believe that the plant form of vitamin A, beta-carotene, can help reduce the risk of developing cancer. A 1981 study of over 2,000 employees of the Western Electric Company in Chicago found that lung cancer rates were lower in smokers who regularly ate beta-carotene-rich vegetables compared to smokers who rarely ate such vegetables. Dr. Pathak, a professor at Harvard Medical School, calls beta-carotene an "oral sunscreen" because it helps to block the harmful effects of the sun's rays in producing skin cancer. The likelihood of an abnormal Pap smear is three times greater for women with diets low in beta-carotene.

According to the most commonly accepted theory today, cancer develops as a two-stage process—initiation and promotion. Initiation is the assault on a healthy cell, causing just a little damage. At this point there is no cancer, just a weak spot where cancer could develop if the second step occurs. This second step is promotion, the development of the damaged cell into a cancerous cell. Various chemicals in the environment—the air, the diet, etc.—can act as either initiators or promoters. Other chemicals, including parts of the diet, can act as anti-promoters. Beta-carotene seems to be an anti-promoter. If it is in a cell, even an "initiated" cell, beta-carotene may be able to stop progress toward cancer by blocking the promotion step.

Vitamin A or beta-carotene from supplements or pills is not always safe. Over-enthusiastic, overdosed pill users have been hospitalized for vitamin A poisoning. A recent research project found that smokers who took beta-carotene pills instead of eating vegetables actually had higher risk for lung cancer. Nor are animal products rich in vitamin A the answer. Liver, meat fat, and eggs are foods to be used only in moderation because they are high in cholesterol and saturated fat. The safest, most abundant source of vitamin A is the plant form found as beta-carotene in vegetables like sweet potatoes. This is why the American Cancer Society recommends eating plenty of fruits and vegetables.

During the past five decades Americans have decreased the amount of beta-carotene they eat because they are eating fewer of the vegetables and fruits that are rich in this nutrient. In the late 1920s Americans were getting 86% of the Daily Value for vitamin A from vegetables such as spinach, sweet potatoes, and carrots. By the 1970s their vitamin A intake from vegetables had dropped to only 76% of the Daily Value.

Certain types of eating patterns in America make the problem more serious. When was the last time you saw sweet potatoes on the menu at a fast food restaurant? How often can you find more than a thimbleful of grated carrots on a fresh salad? Scientists at Pennsylvania State University found that 99% of the customers at fast-food restaurants were getting less than 1/4 of the Daily Value for vitamin A. Why couldn't we have French-fried sweet potatoes as well as French-fried white potatoes?

Sweet Potato Buttermilk Bars

A moist bar with the rich flavor of bygone lazy days.

54 SERVINGS

Nonstick vegetable cooking spray	1 cup all-purpose flour
1/2 cup vegetable shortening	1/2 teaspoon salt
1/4 cup sugar	1/2 teaspoon baking soda
1 egg	1 teaspoon baking powder
1/2 cup molasses	1 teaspoon ginger
1 cup grated raw sweet potato	1 cup whole wheat flour
1 teaspoon grated orange rind	1/4 cup buttermilk*

Preheat oven to 375°. Spray a 9-inch x 13-inch pan with cooking spray and set aside. Cream the shortening and sugar. Add egg and beat thoroughly. Add molasses, sweet potato, and orange rind. Sift together the all-purpose flour, salt, baking soda, baking powder, and ginger. Stir in whole wheat flour. Add dry ingredients alternately with the buttermilk to sweet potato mixture, starting and ending with flour mixture. Spread in prepared pan and bake for 45 to 50 minutes, or until toothpick inserted in center comes out clean. While warm cut into 54 bars (9 by 6).

*TIP: Reconstituted powdered buttermilk can be used.

Nutrition Facts (per serving)

Serving size 1 bar (14g); Servings per recipe 54; Calories 45; Calories from Fat 18; Total Fat 2g (3% DV); Saturated Fat 0; Cholesterol 5mg (2% DV); Vitamin A 14% DV; Vitamin C 1% DV; Sodium 35mg (2% DV); Total Carbohydrate 6g (2% DV); Dietary Fiber 0; Protein 1g; Calcium 1% DV; Iron 2% DV

Yam-Apricot Ice Milk

The name should be "yummy yam"—this dessert is so delicious!

10 SERVINGS

1 1/4 cups cooked, mashed yams
1 cup pureed apricots, fresh or canned
1/3 cup lemon juice

1/2 cup white corn syrup
2 cups low-fat milk (1%)
3/4 cup low-fat whipped topping

Combine yams, apricots, lemon juice, and corn syrup. Mix well. Stir milk into the yam mixture. Fold this mixture into whipped topping and blend thoroughly. Turn into a flat shallow pan and freeze until the mixture is solid about 1 inch from side of pan. Remove from freezer and whip with an electric mixture until light and fluffy. Return to pan and freeze until firm. Makes 1 1/2 quarts. If desired, garnish with a mint leaf and grate a little fresh nutmeg on top as you serve.

Nutrition Facts (per serving)

Serving size 1/2 cup (130g); Servings per recipe 10; Calories 120; Calories from Fat 9; Total Fat 1g (2% DV); Saturated Fat 1g (5% DV); Cholesterol 2mg (1% DV); Vitamin A 108% DV; Vitamin C 17% DV; Sodium 35mg (2% DV); Total Carbohydrate 27g (9% DV); Dietary Fiber 1g (4% DV); Protein 2g; Calcium 7% DV; Iron 1% DV

Yam Waffles with Blueberry Topping

You can't forget them once you've tried them!

12 WAFFLES

3/4 cup whole wheat flour	4 ounces soft tofu
3/4 cup all-purpose flour	1 egg
1/2 cup quick cooking oats	6 ounces mashed yams (or use baby
4 tablespoons sugar	food sweet potatoes)
1/2 teaspoon salt	16 ounces plain nonfat yogurt
1/2 teaspoon cinnamon	1/3 cup vegetable oil
1 tablespoon baking powder	Blueberry Topping (recipe below)

Preheat waffle iron. Stir together the first seven dry ingredients; set aside. In blender or food processor, combine the remaining five ingredients until thoroughly blended. Fold liquid and dry ingredients together. Bake in waffle iron until done, following guidelines of your appliance.

Blueberry Topping

1 1/2 cups water	1/4 teaspoon cinnamon
2 teaspoons sugar	1 pint fresh blueberries*
1 tablespoon cornstarch	1/4 teaspoon grated lemon zest
1/4 teaspoon nutmeg	1/8 teaspoon lemon juice

Put water, sugar, cornstarch, and spices in a heavy saucepan over medium heat. Add blueberries and stir until thickened. Stir in lemon zest and juice. Yields 1 3/4 cups.

TIP: Topping can be made in advance, refrigerated, and reheated for serving.

*TIP: One cup dried blueberries can be substituted.

Nutrition Facts (per serving)

Serving size 1 waffle (150g) with 2 tablespoons topping; Servings per recipe 12; Calories 205; Calories from Fat 72; Total Fat 8g (12% DV); Saturated Fat 1g (5% DV); Cholesterol 24mg (8% DV); Vitamin A 48% DV; Vitamin C 10% DV; Sodium 210mg (9% DV); Total Carbohydrate 29g (10% DV); Dietary Fiber 2g (8% DV); Protein 6g; Calcium 11% DV; Iron 7% DV

Georgia Apple-
Sweet Potato Crunch

Apples and sweet potatoes go together like moonlight and music.

9 SERVINGS

Nonstick vegetable cooking spray

*2 cups cooked, peeled, thinly sliced
sweet potatoes*

*1 1/2 cups cored, peeled, thinly
sliced tart apples*

1/4 cup golden raisins

1/3 cup brown sugar, packed, divided

*3 tablespoons margarine, cut in
pieces*

1/4 teaspoon salt

2 tablespoons margarine, melted

1 cup brown sugar, packed

1/3 cup all-purpose flour

1/2 cup chopped pecans

Preheat oven to 350°. Spray a 2-quart baking dish with cooking spray. Put in half the sweet potatoes and cover with one half of the apples and raisins. Sprinkle with 1/6 cup brown sugar and dot with 1 tablespoon margarine. Add remaining sweet potatoes, apples, and raisins and top with 1/6 cup brown sugar, 2 tablespoons margarine and salt. Cover and bake 30 minutes.

Uncover and bake until the apples are soft (about 30 additional minutes).

Meanwhile in a medium bowl combine the melted margarine, 1 cup brown sugar, flour, and pecans. Sprinkle pecan mixture over the baked dessert and place under a broiler for 1 to 2 minutes, just until top is golden brown. If desired, serve with a dollop of low-fat whipped topping.

Nutrition Facts (per serving)

Serving size 1/2 cup (133g); Servings per recipe 9; Calories 320; Calories from Fat 99; Total Fat 11g (17% DV); Saturated Fat 2g (10% DV); Cholesterol 0; Vitamin A 177% DV; Vitamin C 7% DV; Sodium 190mg (8% DV); Total Carbohydrate 55g (19% DV); Dietary Fiber 2g (8% DV); Protein 2g; Calcium 5% DV; Iron 11% DV

Sweet Pizza

The preteen crowd will enjoy making this snack!

16 SERVINGS

Nonstick vegetable cooking spray

3 cups all-purpose flour

1 teaspoon baking powder

1/8 teaspoon salt

1/3 cup vegetable shortening

2 cups mashed sweet potatoes
(16-ounce can)

3 tablespoons honey

1/2 cup miniature marshmallows

1/2 cup shredded coconut

8 ounces unsweetened pineapple
tidbits, drained

1/8 cup candied cherries, chopped *

Preheat oven to 350°. Lightly spray a 14-inch pizza pan with cooking spray; set aside. Combine flour, baking powder, and salt; cut in shortening until mixture resembles coarse crumbs. Add sweet potatoes and blend well using an electric mixer. Add honey and mix thoroughly. Form dough into a ball and roll onto pizza pan or press with fingers onto pan. Sprinkle marshmallows, coconut, pineapple, and cherries evenly over dough. Bake for 20 minutes or until golden brown. Cool in pan on rack. Cut into wedges and serve.

* TIP: Red candied pineapple can be substituted if cherries are unavailable.

Nutrition Facts (per serving)

Serving size 1 wedge (105g); Servings per recipe 12; Calories 265; Calories from Fat 63; Total Fat 7g (11% DV); Saturated Fat 3g (15% DV); Cholesterol 0; Vitamin A 129% DV; Vitamin C 6% DV; Sodium 95mg (4% DV); Total Carbohydrate 46g (15% DV); Dietary Fiber 2g (8% DV); Protein 4g; Calcium 3% DV; Iron 12% DV

Yamma Banana Swirl

It's so yummy! Why didn't someone think of this before?

12 SERVINGS

1 cup sweet potato puree

2 tablespoons sugar

1 cup banana puree

1 teaspoon lemon juice

1 quart vanilla ice cream, softened

Boil and mash sweet potatoes (or puree in blender or food processor) or purchase baby food sweet potatoes. Stir in sugar. Puree ripe bananas in blender or food processor and add lemon juice. For a swirling ribbon effect in color and taste, swirl sweet potatoes into softened ice cream; put in a flat pan and place in freezer for 20 minutes. Then fold in banana puree and put back in freezer tightly covered.

For a single flavor blend, stir sweet potato and banana mixtures together and then stir into softened ice cream.

Nutrition Facts (per serving)

Serving size 1/2 cup (85g); Servings per recipe 12; Calories 135; Calories from Fat 45; Total Fat 5g (8% DV); Saturated Fat 3g (15% DV); Cholesterol 20mg (7% DV); Vitamin A 68% DV; Vitamin C 5% DV; Sodium 55mg (2% DV); Total Carbohydrate 22g (7% DV); Dietary Fiber 1g (4% DV); Protein 2g; Calcium 7% DV; Iron 2% DV

Sweet Potato Custard Pie

Comfort food that provides an abundance of beta-carotene.

8 SERVINGS

Oatmeal crust (see page 103)

1/4 cup sugar

1/2 teaspoon salt

1/4 teaspoon nutmeg

1 teaspoon orange rind

12-ounce can evaporated skim milk

Water

2 eggs, beaten

2 1/2 cups finely grated raw
*   sweet potato*

1 tablespoon margarine, melted

Prepare Oatmeal Crust, reserving 2 tablespoons oat mixture for topping.

Preheat oven to 425°. In a large mixing bowl, combine sugar, salt, nutmeg, and orange rind. Pour evaporated milk into a 2-cup measure and add water as needed to bring total liquid volume to 1 1/2 cups. Add milk and eggs to sugar mixture and blend well. Add sweet potato and margarine and stir. Pour into Oatmeal Crust and bake for 10 minutes.

Reduce temperature to 350° and continue baking for 30 minutes. Test for doneness by inserting knife halfway between center and edge. Pie is done when knife comes out clean. Sprinkle with reserved oatmeal mixture.

Nutrition Facts (per serving)

Serving size 1 wedge (160g); Servings per recipe 8; Calories 280; Calories from Fat 81; Total Fat 9g (14% DV); Saturated Fat 2g (10% DV); Cholesterol 70mg (23% DV); Vitamin A 252% DV; Vitamin C 21% DV; Sodium 295mg (12% DV); Total Carbohydrate 42g (14% DV); Dietary Fiber 2g (8% DV); Protein 7g; Calcium 16% DV; Iron 7% DV

Maple Sweet Potato Pie

The unique crust adds to the flavor of a great slice of pie.

8 SERVINGS

Cornmeal Crust

1 cup all-purpose flour

1/4 cup cornmeal

1/8 teaspoon salt

1/3 cup vegetable shortening

1/4 cup cold water

Combine flour, cornmeal, and salt. Cut in shortening until mixture resembles coarse crumbs. Add cold water 1 tablespoon at a time, stirring lightly until mixture forms a ball. Roll out on lightly floured surface to form a 13-inch circle. Fit loosely into a 9-inch pie plate; trim. Turn edges under and flute.

Sweet Potato Filling

1 1/2 cups cooked mashed
  sweet potatoes

3/4 cup maple-flavored table syrup

2/3 cup evaporated skim milk

2 eggs

1/4 cup margarine, melted

1 teaspoon vanilla flavoring

1 teaspoon cinnamon

1/4 teaspoon salt

1/4 teaspoon nutmeg

1/4 teaspoon ginger

Preheat oven to 375°. Combine all filling ingredients in large bowl; beat until smooth. Pour into prepared crust. Bake about 45 minutes or until knife inserted in center comes out clean. Serve warm or cold. If desired, add a dollop of low-fat whipped topping for garnish.

Nutrition Facts (per serving)

Serving size 1 wedge (16g); Servings per recipe 8; Calories 375; Calories from Fat 144; Total Fat 16g (25% DV); Saturated Fat 4g (20% DV); Cholesterol 70mg (23% DV); Vitamin A 153% DV; Vitamin C 5% DV; Sodium 260mg (11% DV); Total Carbohydrate 55g (18% DV); Dietary Fiber 2g (8% DV); Protein 6g; Calcium 9% DV; Iron 11% DV

Sweet Potato Cake

A golden ring of delightful flavor and fiber.

12 SERVINGS

Nonstick vegetable cooking spray	2 egg whites
2 cups canned sweet potatoes, drained	2 1/2 cups all-purpose flour
1/2 cup liquid reserved from sweet potatoes	1 teaspoon salt
3/4 cup granulated sugar	1 teaspoon baking soda
1 cup prune puree (recipe below)	1 teaspoon baking powder
1 teaspoon cinnamon	1/2 cup chopped pecans
1/4 cup oil	Orange Icing (recipe below)
1 egg	

Preheat oven to 350°. Spray a 9-inch tube pan with cooking spray and dust with flour; set aside. Mash sweet potatoes with reserved liquid. Stir in sugar, prune puree, cinnamon, and oil. Blend thoroughly. Add egg and egg whites, and beat batter until fluffy. Sift together dry ingredients. Fold into batter carefully. Fold in pecans. Pour batter into prepared pan. Bake for 1 hour and 15 minutes. Cool and frost with Orange Icing.

Prune Puree

Combine 2 2/3 cups (16 ounces) pitted prunes and 3/4 cup water. Put in food processor and pulse on and off until prunes are pureed. Makes 1 cup.

Orange Icing

2 cups sifted powdered sugar	1 tablespoon lemon juice
3 tablespoons margarine	1 tablespoon grated orange rind
3 tablespoons orange juice	Dash of salt

Cream powdered sugar and margarine together. Add remaining ingredients. Beat until smooth and creamy.

Nutrition Facts (per serving)

Serving size 1 piece (160g); Servings per recipe 12; Calories 445; Calories from Fat 99; Total Fat 11g (17% DV); Saturated Fat 2g (10% DV); Cholesterol 23mg (8% DV); Vitamin A 146% DV; Vitamin C 9% DV; Sodium 355mg (15% DV); Total Carbohydrate 84g (28% DV); Dietary Fiber 4g (16% DV); Protein 6g; Calcium 5%; Iron 16%

Sweet Potato Mini Bundt Cakes

A refreshing orange glaze makes this easy-to-fix dessert company fare!

12 SERVINGS

Nonstick vegetable cooking spray	*2 egg whites*
18-ounce package yellow cake mix	*2 cups raw grated sweet potatoes*
1 tablespoon finely grated orange peel	*1/2 cup chopped pecans*
2 teaspoons cinnamon	*2 to 3 teaspoons grated orange peel*
1 1/2 cups unsweetened applesauce	*1 orange, thinly sliced*
1 teaspoon maple flavoring	*3/4 cup pecans*
2 whole eggs	*Glaze (recipes follows)*

Preheat oven to 350°. Spray 12 mini Bundt-style baking cups* with cooking spray and flour lightly; set aside.

In large mixing bowl, combine cake mix, orange peel, cinnamon, applesauce, maple flavoring, eggs, and egg whites. Beat at low speed until moistened, scraping sides and bottom of bowl often. Continue beating at high speed for 2 minutes. Stir in grated sweet potato and pecans. Fill prepared pans 3/4 full. (If using only one 6-cup pan, refrigerate remaining batter until ready to bake.) Bake for 20 to 30 minutes or until toothpick inserted in center comes out clean. Cool on wire rack 5 minutes; remove from pans. Drizzle glaze over warm cakes. To serve, sprinkle additional pecans and 2 to 3 teaspoons grated orange peel over mini-cakes. Cut orange slices in half and place beside each cake on individual serving plates.

*TIP: Cakes can be baked in regular muffin pans. Prepare 28 muffin cups and fill to rim. Bake at 350° for 15 to 20 minutes.

Glaze

1 tablespoon margarine

1/4 cup brown sugar, packed

1/2 cup hazelnut-flavored non-dairy
*   liquid creamer*

1/2 teaspoon maple flavoring

3/4 to 1 cup powdered sugar

1/2 cup chopped pecans

2 to 3 teaspoons grated orange peel

1 orange, thinly sliced

Melt margarine in small saucepan over low heat; stir in brown sugar. Add creamer and cook stirring constantly until mixture is hot and sugar is dissolved. Do not allow to boil! Stir in 1/2 teaspoon maple flavoring and enough powdered sugar for desired consistency. Beat until smooth.

Nutrition Facts (per serving)

Serving size 1 cake (150g); Servings per recipe 12; Calories 330; Calories from Fat 72; Total Fat 8g (12% DV); Saturated Fat 2g (10% DV); Cholesterol 45mg (15% DV); Vitamin A 131% DV; Vitamin C 5% DV; Sodium 35mg (15% DV); Total Carbohydrate 60g (20% DV); Dietary Fiber 2g (8% DV); Protein 4g; Calcium 11% DV; Iron 10% DV

Sweet Potato Kisses

A sincerely sweet kiss with a bit of nutrition.
These candies make an elegant gift.

5 1/2 DOZEN

1/2 medium sweet potato

3 cups powdered sugar

1/2 teaspoon orange extract

Nonstick cooking spray

1/2 teaspoon butter flavoring

2 ounces paraffin wax

6 to 8 ounces German sweet chocolate

Boil sweet potato in salted water until tender; chill in refrigerator overnight. Mash very fine. Add sugar, orange extract, and butter flavoring, making a dough stiff enough to work and shape with hands. Melt chocolate and wax over hot water. Spray hands with cooking spray. Roll dough into balls about the size of quarters, flatten with a fork if desired, and dip into chocolate. Or press dough into a pan and pour chocolate over the top. Store in a tightly covered container.

TIP: If candies are slightly soft, chill before dipping.

Nutrition Facts (per serving)

Serving size 1 piece (6g); Servings per recipe 66; Calories 24; Calories from Fat 0; Total Fat 0; Saturated Fat 0; Cholesterol 0; Vitamin A 4% DV; Vitamin C 0; Sodium 0; Total Carbohydrate 5g (2% DV); Dietary Fiber 0; Protein 0; Calcium 0; Iron 0

Tomatoes

HISTORY

Along with corn and potatoes, the Western Hemisphere gave the world the tomato. The Aztecs cultivated and enjoyed tomatoes for at least a millennium before European explorers came. The conquistadors returned to Europe with tomato seeds. The red globes quickly became an important part of the cuisine of Spain, Portugal, and Italy. When other European peoples began to use the tomato, they gave it nicknames curiously fitting to their own culture. The French called the tomato a "love apple." The Germans noted the apple-like shape and color and called it "the apple of paradise."

Only the British refused to eat this new vegetable. They believed it to be poisonous. A possible reason for the error may be that the tomato vine resembles and is botanically related to the deadly nightshade. Whatever the reason, the English colonists who came to America carried with them the firm belief that tomatoes were toxic. What an ironic twist of fate that although the tomato crossed the Atlantic the first time as a terrific new food, it crossed the Atlantic the second time as a poison not to be eaten!

The American fear of the tomato persisted into the 19th century. In 1781 Thomas Jefferson grew tomatoes in the gardens of Monticello, but not as a food. The plants were merely for decoration! Although Creoles were known to use tomatoes in cooking their spicy gumbos and jambalayas, it wasn't until 1820 that the tomato was proven safe to the satisfaction of the public. On September 26, courageous Colonel Robert G. Johnson stood on the courthouse steps in Salem, New Jersey, and to the horror of onlookers, ate not just one, but a basketful of tomatoes. When he appeared the next morning, not dead and not even sick, the tomato was finally accepted as a wholesome food.

Fruit or vegetable? According to no less an authority than the U.S. Supreme Court the tomato is a vegetable. In 1883 Congress passed a tariff act assessing fees on imported vegetables. Fruits were allowed to enter the country duty-free. The director of customs in New York City collected a tariff on incoming tomatoes, declaring them to be vegetables. The importers claimed they were fruits and filed a lawsuit. When the case finally reached the U.S. Supreme Court, the unanimous decision was

> Botanically speaking tomatoes are the fruit of a vine, just as are cucumbers, squashes, beans and peas. But in the common language of the people… all these are vegetables.

People used to believe that placing a ripe tomato on the mantel when first entering a new home guaranteed future prosperity. Since tomatoes were not available year-round until recently, families moving into new homes often substituted round balls of red fabric stuffed with sawdust or sand. These balls were also used as pincushions, which explains—if you ever wondered—why your grandmother's pincushion looked like a tomato.

OTHER TOMATO LORE AND CLAIMS (WE WON'T VOUCH FOR THE TRUTH OF ANY OF THESE.)

To cure burning feet, place slices of tomato on your feet, wrap, and elevate for 15 minutes.

Treat sunburn with tomatoes soaked in buttermilk. Apply to your skin.

Draw infection from a boil with a warmed slice of tomato.

Problems with skunk odor? Soak in a bath of tomato juice.

Remove garlic and onion odors from your hands with a slice of fresh tomato.

Use tomato juice as a cure for alcohol hangover.

To remove a splinter, sprinkle salt on the area, cover with a small slice of tomato, and hold in place overnight with plastic wrap. In the morning the splinter will pop out.

SEASON

Fresh tomatoes are available year-round, thanks to complementary growing seasons in California and Florida and commercial hothouses. California tomatoes come to our supermarkets May through December. Florida tomatoes are available January through June and again in the autumn.

QUALITY AND STORAGE

A freshly-picked, vine-ripened tomato is a gardener's heavenly reward. Kissed by sunlight, it bursts with a warm flavor like no other. Even if you don't raise your own tomatoes or shop at a local farmer's market, you don't have to settle for a hard supermarket tomato. You can buy fresh tomatoes that are full of flavor. Here's what you need to know.

A fully ripe tomato is red or reddish-orange and has a sweet, subtle aroma. Never squeeze a tomato with your fingers to test ripeness. Hold it in the palm of your hand and gently close your palm around the tomato. A ripe tomato will feel firm yet yield to the gentle pressure of your palm.

Tomatoes pass through six ripening stages from green to pink to full red. They ripen well even if they are picked while still green. The key is keeping them out of the refrigerator to permit full flavor and aroma development. Choose tomatoes that are pink, light red, or red. They will all be equally flavorful and tender when fully ripe. Avoid tomatoes that have soft spots, bruises, or cracks. These are places where decay could easily begin.

Do not refrigerate your tomatoes. Store ripening tomatoes out of the sun, in a cool place (55 to 60°F) such as your basement. Even room temperature is okay but the ripening will be quicker. Tomatoes stored at refrigerator temperatures never reach optimum flavor and texture.

Fresh tomatoes give off ethylene, a gas that is nature's ripener. Tomatoes like company while they ripen. A lone tomato will not ripen as well as a group. A group of tomatoes in a container that can hold the gas, yet is well-vented, will ripen best. For example, ripen tomatoes in a bowl or paper bag.

Ripe tomatoes are highly perishable. If you cannot use them quickly enough, you may store them in a refrigerator for a few days. But flavor and quality will begin to deteriorate.

Storing tomatoes stem end up helps preserve quality. The tomatoes are less easily bruised if they are stored the same way they hang on the plant.

NUTRITIONAL QUALITY

Tomatoes could be the number one source of vitamin A in the American diet. That's not because tomatoes are especially rich in vitamin A. They can't compare to carrots, spinach, and pumpkin. But nearly everyone likes tomatoes. And Americans eat lots of tomatoes—in pizza sauce, spaghetti, salads, and catsup. It may not be a lot of tomato at any one time, but it all adds up.

Like other vegetables, the tomato doesn't contain active vitamin A. It contains one of the plant versions of vitamin A, called as a group "provitamin A carotenoids." Beta-carotene is the most well-known of these carotenoids. Tomatoes are especially rich in a carotenoid called lycopene *(LIE-co-peen)*. In the body, lycopene and other carotenoids are converted to active vitamin A and function in vision, cell development, and immune function. The carotenoids may also act in their own right to maintain good health. They may act as radical scavengers to protect cells, tissues, and organs from damage from environmental contaminants, radiation, and the routine danger of oxidation.

One tomato provides 40% of the Daily Value for vitamin C. It isn't a vitamin C star like the orange or grapefruit, but it makes a big contribution. In fact, the tomato is one of the few vegetables that is a respectable source of vitamin A and vitamin C at the same time, all in one round, red, convenient, natural package.

Green tomatoes have just as much vitamin C and vitamin A as do fully ripe red tomatoes. Flavor, texture, and aroma change, but nutrient content is similar.

The tomato is low in calories, contains no fat or cholesterol and only a small amount of sodium. And the tomato provides some natural fiber.

For an additional dessert incorporating tomatoes, see Habanero Surprise, page 110.

Don's Soft Molasses Cookies

*One of our recipe testers was raised on these cookies. He continues
the tradition of creating them with love and adds a little more nutrition.*

36 SERVINGS

Nonstick vegetable cooking spray	*1 1/2 teaspoons salt*
1 cup sugar	*1 teaspoon baking soda*
1/2 cup shortening	*1 1/2 teaspoons ginger*
1 cup dark molasses	*1/2 teaspoon cloves*
1/2 cup water	*1/2 teaspoon nutmeg*
1/2 cup tomato puree	*1/4 teaspoon allspice*
4 cups all-purpose flour	*Granulated sugar for tops*

Preheat oven to 350°. Spray cookie sheets with cooking spray and set aside. In
large mixing bowl, blend sugar and shortening. Add molasses, water, and tomato
puree and thoroughly mix. Sift together dry ingredients; fold into molasses mixture and stir until well blended. Drop by teaspoonfuls onto prepared sheets.
Sprinkle with sugar. Bake for 10 to 15 minutes. Makes 6 dozen 2-inch cookies.

Nutrition Facts (per serving)

Serving size 2 cookies (35g); Servings per recipe 36; Calories 115; Calories from Fat
27; Total Fat 3g (5% DV); Saturated Fat 1g (5% DV); Cholesterol 0 ; Vitamin A
1% DV; Vitamin C 2% DV; Sodium 120mg (5% DV); Total Carbohydrate 21g
(7% DV); Dietary Fiber 1g (4% DV); Protein 2g; Calcium 6% DV; Iron 16% DV

Sliced Green Tomato Pie

A gardener's gourmet dessert.

8 SERVINGS

4 cups peeled, thinly sliced
  green tomatoes

1 1/4 cups sugar

1/2 teaspoon cinnamon

1/2 teaspoon nutmeg

1/4 teaspoon salt

4 tablespoons flour

2 tablespoons lemon juice

Pastry for two-crust pie

Preheat oven to 425°. To peel tomatoes: Immerse in boiling water (about 3 minutes), loosen, then submerge in ice water. Remove skin. Slice with a serrated edge knife to achieve thin slices.

In a large bowl blend together sugar, cinnamon, nutmeg, salt, flour, and lemon juice. Add green tomatoes and toss. Place one of the pastries in a 9-inch pie pan. Add the tomato mixture. Cover with top crust, flute edges, and cut vents. Bake until tomatoes are soft and crust is lightly browned, about 50 to 60 minutes.

Nutrition Facts (per serving)

Serving size 1 wedge (170g); Servings per recipe 8; Calories 340; Calories from Fat 108; Total Fat 12g (18% DV); Saturated Fat 3g (15% DV); Cholesterol 0; Vitamin A 21% DV; Vitamin C 29% DV; Sodium 400mg (17% DV); Total Carbohydrate 56g (19% DV); Dietary Fiber 2g (8% DV); Protein 4g; Calcium 3% DV; Iron 10% DV

Apple-Tomato Pie

The apple and green tomato complement each other superbly.

8 SERVINGS

2 cups thinly sliced green tomatoes

3 cups thinly sliced tart cooking
   apples, peeled

2/3 cup brown sugar, firmly packed

1/3 cup granulated sugar

1/2 teaspoon cinnamon

1/8 teaspoon salt

2 to 3 tablespoons flour

1 tablespoon butter or margarine

Pastry for two-crust pie

Preheat oven to 425°. Immerse in boiling water (about 3 minutes), loosen, then submerge in ice water. Remove skin. Slice with a serrated knife to achieve thin slices easily. In large bowl blend together sugars, cinnamon, salt, and flour. Add green tomatoes and apple slices and toss gently to mix. Place one of the pastries in a 9-inch pie pan. Add the apple mixture. Dot filling with butter. Cover with top crust, flute edges, and cut vents. Bake until tomatoes and apples are soft and crust is lightly browned, about 50 to 60 minutes.

Nutrition Facts (per serving)

Serving size 1 wedge (175g); Servings per recipe 8; Calories 345; Calories from Fat 117; Total Fat 13g (20% DV); Saturated Fat 3g (15% DV); Cholesterol 0; Vitamin A 15% DV; Vitamin C 21% DV; Sodium 385mg (16% DV); Total Carbohydrate 54g (18% DV); Dietary Fiber 3g (12% DV); Protein 3g; Calcium 4% DV; Iron 12% DV

Snappy Tomato and Spice Cake

An old favorite that's been updated for today's light cooking and eating.

24 SERVINGS

Nonstick vegetable cooking spray

2 cups all-purpose flour

1 1/3 cups sugar

4 teaspoons baking powder

1 teaspoon baking soda

1 1/2 teaspoons allspice*

1 teaspoon cinnamon

1/2 teaspoon ground cloves

10 3/4-ounce can condensed tomato soup

1/2 cup applesauce

2 eggs

1/4 cup water

Light Cream Cheese Icing (below)

Preheat oven to 350°. Spray a 9-inch x 13-inch pan with cooking spray and set aside. Measure dry ingredients into a large bowl. Add soup and applesauce. Beat at medium speed for 2 minutes, scraping sides and bottom of bowl. Add eggs and water. Beat another 2 minutes, scraping bowl frequently. Pour batter into pan. Bake for 35 to 40 minutes. Cool and frost with Light Cream Cheese Icing.

*TIP: If you prefer a milder spice flavor, omit the allspice and replace it with 1/2 teaspoon nutmeg.

Light Cream Cheese Icing

2 cups powdered sugar

1/2 of 8-ounce tub light cream cheese

1 tablespoon skim milk

1 teaspoon vanilla extract

Cream together all ingredients until smooth.

Nutrition Facts (per serving)

Serving size 1 piece (55g); Servings per recipe 24; Calories 140; Calories from Fat 18; Total Fat 2g (3% DV); Saturated Fat 1g (5% DV); Cholesterol 25mg (8% DV); Vitamin A 3% DV; Vitamin C 11% DV; Sodium 190mg (8% DV); Total Carbohydrate 30g (10% DV); Dietary Fiber 1g (4% DV); Protein 2g; Calcium 2% DV; Iron 4%

Turnips

HISTORY

The turnip was first used by the peoples who found it growing wild in the sandy soils of the Northern European coastal plains. An important sustaining food of the ancient Gauls and Germanic tribes, the turnip was quickly adopted by the colonizing Romans.

Turnips are the star in a favorite Roman story. Curius Dentatus was consul in 290-275 BC. He rose to political power after being a hero in the wars with neighboring Latin tribes, during which Republican Rome consolidated its power and supremacy. After his term as consul ended, unlike so many politicians, he retired happily to his farm. One day envoys from the Samnites, a hostile tribe, arrived at the farm and attempted to bribe Dentatus to lead them against the dominant Romans. As it happens, the agents arrived when Dentatus was engaged in the homely business of roasting turnips over a fire. A true hero to the end, Dentatus turned them away, saying he preferred his humble turnips to treacherous gold.

A white turnip is the star of another tale from ancient times. Nicomedes, king of Bithynia (present-day northern Turkey), was very fond of the pilchard, a sardine-like fish. One day when the king requested pilchard for dinner, the cook was unable to obtain any from the fishermen. Since no request of a king can be denied, the imaginative cook carved a white turnip into the shape of a pilchard, baked it, and served it on the traditional fish platter. While the cook waited nervously in the kitchen, the king devoured the "fish" and pronounced it the best fish he had ever eaten.

The importance of turnips declined after a time, but during the disruptions of the Middle Ages in Europe—the plague, wars, and crop failures—the turnip came back into favor as a hedge against famine. It remained a major food for humans until explorers returned from the New World with the potato, at which time it declined in popularity.

While country folk used the turnip to avoid starvation, at banquets of the wealthy, turnips were beautifully carved into fantastic centerpieces: turreted castles, steepled churches, and ships with billowing sails.

It was long a country tradition for a young woman to give a young man a turnip to show him she was no longer interested in his attentions. From this practice came the phrase, "to give him a turnip," meaning to reject him. Turnips have been thrown by unruly crowds to insult speakers or actors. Turnips even turn up in that old saying, little heard today, referring to an impossible feat, "you can't get blood from a turnip."

There are many varieties, colors, and sizes among turnips, including white, red, yellow, gray, and almost black-fleshed. The so-called Swedish turnip is not a turnip at all, but a rutabaga and a member of the cabbage family.

SEASON

Fresh turnips are available all year because, like most root crops, they store well. However, freshly-harvested turnips are in season from May through January, with the peak coming in late fall.

QUALITY AND STORAGE

Look for turnips that are firm and heavy for their size. Skin should be smooth, not shriveled, and unblemished. If the green tops are still attached, they should still be crisp and deep green. Although turnips can grow to massive sizes, the smaller ones are sweeter and more tender.

Like most other root vegetables, turnips are champion keepers under the right conditions—cool, dry, dark locations. At home, keep fresh turnips in a plastic bag in the crisper drawer of the refrigerator. They will maintain good quality for at least a week and perhaps longer.

NUTRITIONAL QUALITY

The turnip's nutrient content mirrors the more familiar white potato with two exceptions. The turnip is considerably lower in calories and higher in calcium. At a cost of only 21 calories, 1/2 cup of cooked, mashed turnip provides 3% of the Daily Value for calcium, 22% of the Daily Value for vitamin C, and 5% of the Daily Value for folate. While the humble turnip does not single-handedly meet 100% of your need for any nutrient, it can certainly contribute, along with other foods, to the nutrients that you need daily for best health. Virtually fat free and exceptionally low in calories, the turnip is especially valuable when it takes the place of high-calorie ingredients in meals and recipes.

Streusel Turnip Pie

A real surprise from a bountiful garden or the farmer's market.
Just don't say what the ingredient is until the eater tells you it's good!

8 SERVINGS

4 cups peeled, thinly sliced turnips

1 cup sugar

2 tablespoons flour

1 teaspoon cinnamon

1/4 teaspoon ground nutmeg

1/4 teaspoon salt

1/2 teaspoon cream of tartar

2 tablespoons vanilla flavoring

2 tablespoons fresh lemon juice

9-inch prepared deep-dish pie shell,
   homemade, frozen, or refrigerated

1/3 cup margarine, softened

1/2 cup sugar

1 cup all-purpose flour

1/2 teaspoon grated lemon rind

Preheat oven to 400°. Slice turnips very thin with a food processor or a sharp knife. In a stainless steel pan* precook turnips in enough water to cover for 5 to 7 minutes. Or, cook in microwave oven for 9 to 11 minutes. Drain and cool. In a large bowl mix together 1 cup sugar, 2 tablespoons flour, and seasonings; stir in vanilla extract and lemon juice and mix thoroughly. Stir in turnips and put mixture into pie shell. In a small bowl cut 1/3 cup margarine into 1/2 cup sugar, 1 cup flour, and 1/2 teaspoon grated lemon rind to make a streusel. Sprinkle streusel over pie. Bake for 20 minutes; reduce heat to 350° and bake an additional 20 to 30 minutes, or until streusel has warm brown highlights.

*TIP: Aluminum or iron cookware may cause the turnips to discolor.

Nutrition Facts (per serving)

Serving size 1 wedge (170g); Servings per recipe 8; Calories 400; Calories from Fat 135; Total Fat 15g (23% DV); Saturated Fat 3g (15% DV); Cholesterol 0; Vitamin A 6% DV; Vitamin C 18% DV; Sodium 330mg (14% DV); Total Carbohydrate 65g (22% DV); Dietary Fiber 3g (12% DV); Protein 4g; Calcium 3% DV; Iron 9% DV

Index